LETTERS TO CHRISTIAN LEADERS

LETTERS TO CHRISTIAN LEADERS

JAKE FARR-WHARTON

dangerous™
little books

First Published in Great Britain 2011
by Dangerous Little Books www.dangerouslittlebooks.com

To my two breathtakingly beautiful, sublimely intelligent, delirium inducing daughters; question everything... except me... and your mother.

To my darling American wife; I'll never question you... I freaking swear.

To the religious world; it's important to have an open mind, but not to such a degree that your brain falls out.

To my fellow rationalists, freethinkers, atheists and naturalists; apathy and religious leaders are our enemies, not the religious sheeple. Help them to see their leaders and doctrines for what they are, but without proselytizing... god damn it, now I'm proselytizing!

Contents

Introduction

Since the publication of my book, *'God Hates You. Hate Him Back'*, I have been involved in countless enthralling religious debates, both online and offline, and have an inbox overflowing with messages from angry Christians to show for it. Admittedly, not all of the emails are of the 'Burn in Hell mo-fo' kind, but most do fall into the 'I pray that Jesus is merciful on your soul when you meet him in Heaven' category. And if there's anything more condescending and more irksome to me personally then I'm yet to find it.

Actually, my favorite email was from a guy who said "you'll regret writing that book when you arrive in Hell and Satan forces you to suck his shriveled member for all eternity". I always laugh when Christians play the 'eternity card', as though eternity is a concept that only their (or my) feeble little brain can fathom. The universe has not existed for eternity, nor will it. All things are finite. Fact!

Notwithstanding the number of copies my book has sold or, moreover, the success' of the champions of reason and those whose intellect surely towers over mine, including Messers Dawkins, Hitchens, Dennet, and Harris – the numbers of people moving away from, or at least questioning, irrational beliefs, so as to arrive at secular reason, continues only at a trickle. Simply, the message is getting out there, but it isn't being bought. This book's objective is to make that sale.

The best way for atheists to help one another deal with our respective Jesus guzzling buddies is by arming ourselves with argumentative ammunition that completely refutes the all too predictable and script like theistic arguments... with unpredictable non-script like atheist arguments. Better yet, why not target the leaders! Effectively, implementing the same policy adopted by that US Marine Lieutenant, who commented at the conclusion of the street battle in Hue during the Tet Offensive, "We had to raze the city in order to save it." In the same manner, Jake takes a match and lights the Christian argument to shreds (mixed metaphors are fun). The next time a LDS, J-Dub or Christian McFundy knocks on your door, you will be equipped to graciously extend an invitation to your lounge room and just as they conclude their canned 'Jesus became my personal Lord and Savior', you will be heading to the nearest strip club with your new white shirt, black tie, magic under-pant wearing buddies to celebrate their conversion to a little place we like to call RATION-FREAKING-ALITY!

Rational thought, meticulous reasoning and scientific evidence will always be your best ammunition against theists... well, that and being able to cherry-pick all the best shit from the Bible! By the end of this book, you will be a jihadist for rationalism; a martyr for secularism; a pastor of reason; a minister of skepticism; and ultimately a warrior for peace and human solidarity… or at the very least, you'll be able to stand up to religious ignorance and injustice in society and in the workplace.

See, here's the thing: Our earth is little more than a tiny planet in this great solar system, in this immense galaxy in this seemingly infinite universe. We're objectively insignificant to the universe, but we're in turmoil. No shit! For the last 2000 years and more, we've stripped this planet of resource after resource all in the name of progress, ultimately, to mark our place in time. Meanwhile, the place is getting warmer, the wars are getting 'Bushier' and there is more emphasis on how thick your hair is, how sweet your cereal tastes, and your ability to maintain a healthy erection, than on creating clean power, clean transport and universal healthcare.

Why? There exists this stupid notion that life is just your opportunity to impress God with your good deeds, enough so that he'll let you into Heaven, paradise, Valhalla, or some other magical place where horny virgins or housewives reign supreme. By increasing the number of socially, environmentally and culturally aware atheists, anti-theists, skeptics, secularists, and agnostics on this planet, then we will finally be able to shift our attention towards improving social wellbeing.

In secular Holland, we've already seen how attention towards equality, education and healthcare has reduced crime, lowered disease, whereby increasing the general quality of life for all... not to mention, those particular secularists are some of the most sublimely attractive people north of Australia! We will expand on all of these assertions throughout this book.

Mostly, this book targets the happy clapper evangelical Christian conservatives, primarily in America (but popping up all the time in the UK, in Australia, and even Korea, Japan and China), because quite frankly, this group represents the American equivalent of the socially despotic Taliban. If this bunch of socially and culturally ignorant lunatics aren't muddying the waters in effort to camouflage the line that separates Church and State; then they are lobbying for Intelligent Design (or worse, Genesis Creationism) to be taught, side-by-side with Evolution, in Schools as equally viable and acceptable theories; they block stem cell research initiatives; they actively target and discriminate against homosexuals; they deny the right to die with dignity through voluntary euthanasia, regardless of one's wishes; they legislate away from environmental preservation because "God will take care of it"; or at the far fringe, they bomb abortion clinics and kill doctors that perform them.

While you may well think these people 'easy targets', they are the ones making the most noise; they are the ones recruiting the most followers and the ones teaching humanity to circumvent logic, reason and evidence in place of faith... eww!

Even in 2011, those who don't believe a deity was somehow responsible for the creation of the Universe number below 15%, while still more than 50% of Americans believe in the literal translation of the Bible. As Sam Harris pointed out in his book *Letters to a Christian Nation*, this means that today circa 150 million Americans believe vehemently that God created the world 1,000 years after the Sumerians had invented glue (and most likely around the time that the authors of the Old Testament were sniffing said glue).

Consider that in 2011, 150 million Americans and billions worldwide maintain the ancient belief that humanity was saved and then repopulated by a 900 year old man named Noah and the two of every kind of animals he brought along for the ride. Seriously, how many ultra-senior citizens do you know that have the stamina to usher two of every species onto a boat before encouraging them to have sex at sea for the 150 days the love boat stayed adrift? Wouldn't you think someone that old would be spending most of their remaining energy FIGHTING DECOMPOSITION?

We're talking millions of people who believe that the fossil record and dinosaurs are a trick that God played on humanity to make them stray from His word. In other words, they believe facts were created by the Devil to test one's faith.

If you believe that the Bible is the infallible word of God, and that god is an awesome dude with a big fluffy beard, then this bookarooni, neighbourino, is for you! Nations, for too long have tolerated these stupid, ignorant and the downright intolerant beliefs! It is high time that people like you start combating this slice of the populace as their ignorance is positively viral!

Let us not forget that their so called 'Holy Books' foster a moronic form of morality; an inept form of human solidarity; a convoluted sense of what is good for the world and; by their very nature, abhor critical thinking.

If humanity truly wishes to move forward as a civilization, we cannot allow someone with a vehement belief that they will see Jesus' return within their lifetime to control our weapons of mass destruction (and not just because it is an utterly ridiculous belief). Seriously, if your Bible or Qur'an or Torah tells you that killing infidels is noble, and you believe it with all the impetuosity of a fundamentalist such as Bush or Ahmadinejad – and we can only imagine what would have happened if trigger happy Palin and McCain had won... but there's still 2012. Why would you refrain from pressing the RED go button if you believed a nuclear winter held the secret to the promise of the end of times?

The various holy books provide 21st century mankind no intrinsic or altruistic benefit whatsoever. There is nothing within these texts that provides us with a profound source of inspiration to solve any societal ills, or indeed the wisdom to advance our civilization into the future. In fact, these texts only serve to fan the flames of social dysfunction, providing us with a rear view mirror to an age when the metal axe was thought to be emergent technology and it was cool to stone someone to death.

The last 400 years have seen remarkable breakthroughs in our understanding of the universe and how we came to be here. If you spread the message, or take up the cause, we offer solace that your children won't be taught that the answer to everything is simply, "God did it, don't ask again." We offer a chance for you to be, rightfully, proudly and openly an atheist without being ostracized by co-workers, teammates or peers and being thought of as an unremarkable minority by your politicians.

After all, how free can someone truly be if they believe they are being supervised 24/7 - even in their sleep - by a being that may convict you for something as freaking mundane as a thought crime (thou shall not covet thy neighbor's crap)?

It was secularists who founded the great Nation of the USA. It was secularists who abolished slavery in the 19th Century. It will be secularists who save America from itself, by saving her from bludgeoning the intellectual and social development of tomorrow's children.

Not just America though, every nation, the world over, has been suffering from an extreme case of religious literalism and fundamentalism.

But for all these rich, idealistic and altruistic objectives to become attainable the secularists must make themselves known and they must metaphorically carpet bomb the bejesus out of every potential argumentative hiding place that theists retreat to. Smoke them out of their holes. All bridges to retreat must be burnt behind them, and when that happens, our goal for progress, in America and the rest of the world, will be driving in the right direction.

I believe this book acts as the bunker buster bomb for winning the war against irrational, illogical, nonsensical and non-evidence based belief systems. Jake has written each chapter in the form of a letter addressed to those who make the respective arguments that support those belief systems, and the many ridiculous dogmas that spawn from them. I believe this book counters most of the arguments that theists put forward, as their arguments tend to follow a predictable structured script. No better illustrated than the fact that the Kirk Cameron's of the world are training Christian children how to challenge biology teachers by peeling a bloody banana. I wish I were making this up. I'm not!

Be warned that the language is condescending in parts and downright puerile and mischievous in others. How else should one respond to a believer who is so arrogantly certain in his or her belief that he or she has unlocked the key to the supernatural but you are too blind or stupid to realize it? This is about giving them a taste of their own medicine. Empiricism will prevail.

CJ Werleman
Author of 'God Hates You. Hate Him Back'
and 'Jesus Lied. He Was Only Human'
www.cjwerleman.com

TO ROBERTA COMBS

Gays, Abortions & Tax Cuts – It's Not Cool To Be A Republican

Dear Reader, the following address is from Roberta Combs, President of the Christian Coalition of America (CCOA). Here she discusses the agenda for CCOA. The CCOA, loudly and proudly, provides a conservative Christian voice for Christian Americans. It acts as a Christian lobby group, fighting to ensure that the separation of church and state is relegated to fairytale stories. The full address can be found at: *www.cc.org/2010_legislative_agenda.*

Barack Obama promised Planned Parenthood that he would sign FOCA, and we have to take him at his word and work to prevent its passage. FOCA would actually abolish such federal laws as the ban on the abominable practice of partial-birth abortion, in addition to voiding hundreds of state and local laws and regulations on abortion. It is the most radical piece of pro-abortion legislation ever proposed in our country.

It will be a top priority of the Christian Coalition of America to stop the "Freedom of Choice Act" and continue our fight to defend the unborn.

We support the nomination and confirmation of judges that will uphold and apply the Constitution as it was originally written by our Founding Fathers – not seek to re-write it to their own ideological ends, or make law from the bench.

Christian Coalition will be monitoring all of the judicial nominations sent to the United States Senate by President Obama. We will be happy to support nominees that abide by a philosophy of applying the original understanding of our Constitution. And we will stand in firm opposition to the confirmation of all who do not.

It seems that everywhere you look, the traditional definition of marriage is under attack as liberals seek to radically redefine an institution that has existed for thousands of years. In recent years it has come under attack by left-wing judges who have sought to redefine marriage by judicial decree. And now, Barack Obama has indicated that he favors repealing the 1996 Defense of Marriage Act.

The Defense of Marriage Act is a federal law that prohibits the federal government from treating "same sex" relationships as marriage, and prevents states from being required to give legal recognition to gay marriages performed in other states. Christian Coalition will aggressively oppose any efforts to overturn the Defense of Marriage Act.

Christian Coalition will fight to prevent any re-introduction of the so-called "Fairness Doctrine" from taking effect, (whether in the form of Congressional legislation or government regulation).

The "Fairness Doctrine" – which would have the practical effect of forcing radio and TV stations to broadcast an equal amount of time for liberal programs to match that of each conservative program – was abolished in the 1980's by former President Ronald Reagan. If it is allowed to come back, it would effectively end conservative talk-radio and put Christian television programming at risk.

With so many promising new developments in the area of adult stem-cell research, there is absolutely no reason whatsoever for the government to continue to allow – much less expand – funding for research and destruction of embryonic stem-cells. Despite this fact, the Obama administration and the Democrat leadership in Congress have made plain that they will attempt to do just that.

Christian Coalition will work to defeat any measures that expand embryonic stem-cell research and spotlight all members of Congress who support using taxpayer dollars for this abominable practice.

Christian Coalition worked to help former President Bush pass legislation that lowered federal taxes for virtually every family in America by a total of $1.3 trillion, (a bill which passed by a large bipartisan margin in the 107th Congress).

Unfortunately, the tax cuts are set to expire in 2010. Christian Coalition will work to defend those tax cuts and protect the income of America's family's from rising taxes under Barack Obama's administration.

Even though a federal court during October 2006 dismissed gadfly Mikey Weinstein's infamous lawsuit which accused the United States military of promoting Christianity, he filed yet a new lawsuit less than two months later, wasting American taxpayer dollars yet again. He is trying to force the Pentagon into wasting more time to check into his allegations. Undoubtedly, another federal court judge will strike down his latest exercise in futility and harassment of Christians in the United States military.

Christian Coalition of America will fight to ensure that evangelical Christian military chaplains and other personnel are not discriminated against as they have been during the past number of decades. In the closing weeks of the 109th Congress, Republican congressional leaders got involved in this culture war and forced the Navy and the Air Force to repeal regulations the two services had adopted earlier this year which forbade military chaplains from praying in the name of Jesus during military functions other than worship services. The provision agreed to on September 25, 2006 by the House and Senate conferees debating the final Defense Authorization bill rolls back the current Air Force and Navy regulations which had overturned 200+ years of tradition allowing military chaplains to pray in the name of Jesus and according to their faith requirements. The Air Force had adopted restrictive guidelines on February 9, 2006 and the Navy had adopted similar restrictive guidelines on February

21, 2006. The Air Force and Navy had surrendered to atheist activists and left-wing Members of Congress in adopting these ill-advised regulations.

According to the September 25, 2006 agreement signed by the House and Senate conferees, the Secretary of the Air Force must reinstate the policy that was set forth in Air Force Directive 52-1 dated 1 July 1999 and the Secretary of the Navy must reinstate the policy set forth in Secretary of Navy Instruction 1730.7B dated October 12, 2000.

Dear Roberta,

It's a beautiful thing when things 'just work', isn't it? You work tirelessly on a project and it integrates and performs perfectly; or you train for months to compete in a triathlon and, consequently, you're able to obliterate your old personal best time; or you find that the batteries to your wife's vibrator perfectly fit the TV remote. All in all, it is just great when things work the way that they should!

When Barak Obama was elected to the presidency of the United States of America, the world breathed a sigh of relief. Around the world, rational men and women laughed and cried in joy.

It wasn't just because we all thought that Barak would be the savior of the world, a Black Super Man, either. No, the day that Barak Obama was elected, we rejoiced because Sarah Palin, and whoever the other old dude was, were defeated by Obama and Biden on a platform of 'change, for the better' under the awe inspiring catchphrase, "YES WE CAN!"

The election proved, once and for all, that if enough rational people stand up to vote on polling day, the Christian conservative vote can be circumvented.

4

In democratic countries, we elect our government based on what they say they will do, and hope that throughout their term in power, they'll do as promised. They are cognizant of the fact that if they do a poor job, if they squander the cash reserves, alienate a large enough group of people or step on too many toes, they simply won't get re-elected. Or will they?

Many people have, for one reason or another, forgotten the year or so that George "Sir Wankalot" Bush Jr and Al Gore spent in the High Court in an attempt to procure the presidency. Gore had actually won the popular vote by 500,000 odd votes, but Sir Wankalot, his oil money and his excitable daddy prevailed over Gore (I hope you'll excuse the gross oversimplification). It was a travesty that resulted in eight years of mismanagement, reckless spending, and devaluing America's reputation and culminated in a prolonged and poorly handled war on Iraq and Afghanistan in retaliation for a meticulously constructed terrorist attack that we all remember as 9/11.

As an objective observer, I was utterly amazed at how well Bush and his team played the re-election.

> "Twenty-eight months have passed since September 11, 2001 - over two years without an attack on American soil - and it is tempting to believe that the danger is behind us," Mr Bush said. "That hope is understandable, comforting - and false."
> (George Bush in January, 2004).

Bush royally ass-raped America for eight long, and excruciatingly painful years... all without reprieve... or lubrication. He obliterated the economy, he sent men and women off to die on his quasi-religious crusade and he enacted a profound detriment upon the education system of America.

He did all of this on a strong platform of 'Christian Values'.

Don't let yourself be fooled. Everything that Bush did, he did in the name of his God, the Christian God:

"I believe that God wants everybody to be free. That's what I believe. And that's part of my foreign policy. In Afghanistan, I believe that the freedom there is a gift from the Almighty." (October, 2004)

Much like the popes and kings of the past, or even the terrorists who flew planes into buildings, Bush believed that he was doing what God thought was best:

"I am driven with a mission from God. God would tell me, 'George go and fight these terrorists in Afghanistan'. And I did. And then God would tell me 'George, go and end the tyranny in Iraq'. And I did." (George Bush, August, 2003)

So if you ever wonder why the minority of intelligent, rational, free-thinking, atheists/agnostics that live in America are so vocal about the role of religion in politics and the separation of church and state, it is because it is quite obviously dangerous.

A fundamental problem that we face is the fact religion is inherently divisive and inherently delusional. When one speaks of one's religion, there is a very good reason why one is unable to speak either logically or rationally, for belief without evidence is illogical and irrational. This does not, of course, mean that religion is inherently bad, it just means that religious prejudice, religious ideology and segregation (whether intentionally imposed or not) is not based on any rational or evidence based reason, but on fairytales and fables.

It is one thing for an average and fairly unimportant member of the public to believe that we all live under the supervision of a mystical overlord who judges one and all for their piety, belief and servitude after death. It is another thing entirely to put that delusional person in charge of the largest stockpile of weapons of mass destruction on Earth.

Bush screwed millions of children out of an adequate education, and still thinks he's going to Heaven when he dies. Bush's actions and inactions forced hundreds of thousands to lose their jobs, close their businesses and foreclose on their homes, and he still believes he's going to Heaven when he dies. Bush took several days to send people and aid to New Orleans after successive hurricanes devastated and flooded everything, which directly contributed to the unconscionable number of deaths, and he still believes he's going to Heaven when he dies. Bush sent thousands of citizens of the United States of America to die in places and situations he had not gained intelligence in (he had no idea what the difference between a Sunni and Shiite Muslims were), against an ideology he did not understand, and still, he believes he is going to Heaven.

There is a fundamental problem, when the people of a nation (likely driven by an overly propagandizing media) value religious affiliation and supposed 'values', over substance of policy. Thankfully, enough of the left came out to vote in '08 and got a Progressive into the presidency. Obama will never have the time, or support, even if given two full terms to fix the incredible damage that a certain Christian Conservative Republican and his trigger-happy friends did.

Nonetheless, the message is clear; no person, alive or dead, (or zombified in Jesus' case) should be weighed based on his or her religious piety. It is neither an accurate measure of worth, nor an indication of suitability. Religion tears people apart, it divides nations, suburbs, streets and houses, is there any wonder why an openly religious and fundamentalist president turned out to be the ruin of the United States of America?

Now to your policy.

On Abortion and Sex Education for Young People
Most people make the choice to abort a fetus not because they are medically compelled to do so; they have abortions because they did not properly consider the consequences of unprotected sex. The fact is, Roberta, if you want abortions to stop, you need to teach about the unintended consequences of sex. People need to be taught about condoms, about birth control, about STIs and STDs and pregnancy.

Do you oppose the use of condoms, Roberta? Are you one of those puritans who say that sex should strictly be for procreation? Obviously, this makes sense when your partner is boring in bed, but might I suggest the Karma Sutra... or even some good old fashioned sodomy (check the meaning in the dictionary before you cringe)!

The Freedom of Choice Act is a huge step in allowing freedom of choice to teenagers all over America who were denied an adequate sexual education whilst at school under Bush's "Abstinence Only" sex education legislation. Obama, realizing this major failing on Bush's part, repealed this legislation and allocated funding for research into better equipping the next generation with a more adequate sexual education.

Honestly, the most naive position that any parent can ever take is to assume that their child will not try to have sex at their first opportunity to do so. Sex is as ubiquitous a part of being a teenager as driving fast and getting sick after smoking an oregano joint because your friend said it was just as good as weed. It is just part of growing up and to expect otherwise either demonstrates your inability to remember your own youth, or worse, that you had a horribly boring teenage experience.

That said, you show any teenage boy a couple of pictures of swollen, pus and sore covered male members and I guarantee you they'll look at sex in a completely different way… they might even use a condom.

Nonetheless, sex for teens has always been, and will always be just another of the laws of nature. After all, it is just another biological urge produced by our evolutionary compulsion to reproduce like rabbits (or go forth and multiply)!

So, does abstinence only sex-ed work? Well, the answer is a resounding NO!

- 94% of all Texas school districts teach abstinence-only sex-ed, with only 3% teaching abstinence-plus (abstinence plus condoms and other forms of birth control).

- Fifty-six percent of high school students in Texas report having used condoms at last intercourse.

Only three states have lower rates of condom use among students.

- Texas' teen pregnancy rate of 101 pregnancies per 1,000 girls ages 15-19 is significantly higher than the national rate of 84. Only four states have higher teen pregnancy rates than Texas. Since 1990, Texas' pregnancy rate has dropped by 18 percent, compared to a 24 percent drop nationwide.

- Texas' teen birth rate of 62 births per 1,000 girls ages 15-19 is the highest in the nation – significantly higher than the national rate of 41. Since 1990, Texas' birth rate has dropped by 21 percent, compared to a 34 percent drop nationwide.

- Texas' AIDS case rate of 13 cases per 100,000 people is the tenth highest, worse than 40 states. Among 45 states with HIV reporting, Texas has the third highest number (24,699) of people living with HIV.

- Young people ages 15-24 comprised twenty percent of Texas' new HIV cases in 2006.

- Texas' youth, especially young women, are at risk for STIs:

  o Youth ages 15-24 experienced 73 percent of the total number of Chlamydia cases in Texas in 2006.

  o Youth ages 15-24 experienced 61 percent of the total number of Gonorrhea cases in Texas in 2006.

o For all youth in this age range, young women were most at risk for STIs, experiencing 83 percent of Chlamydia infections and 60 percent of gonorrhea infections.

So the resounding message, Roberta, is that teaching abstinence is 100% effective when used... but in reality only works on no one, exactly none of the time.

This has a direct economic impact as well:

Consider that nationally, nearly one million young women under age 20 become pregnant each year. That means close to 2800 teens get pregnant each day. Approximately 4 in 10 young women in the U.S. become pregnant at least once before turning 20 years old. Teen childbearing alone costs U.S. taxpayers nearly $7 billion annually for social services and lost tax revenues. These figures were from a 1996 study and since no further comprehensive studies having been performed since, we can only assume that these figures have spiraled further and further in the last 14 years.

The huge proportion (but by no means all) of these children having children will keep their subsequent children in a cycle of poverty and poor education that will ensure the next generation is subjected to the exact same cycle. Thus the focus for you preachy nitpickers should be on adequately educating children how to, when they're ready, have sex, safely. This will carry through their teens and into their twenties and thirties until they're ready to have children.

Sex is bloody brilliant, it is so much fun, it feels great (once you know how to do it) and it is perfectly natural, no matter what your sexual orientation. So, the message is, don't make kids feel bad for having urges, help them to do what they're going to do anyway, safely!

That said, people will always make stupid mistakes (which is exactly what an unwanted pregnancy is). As such, abortion should always be an option that is available to all, regardless of age, race or religious background.

Having a child will completely alter the life of a young person for the rest of their life. Forget education, career, social and love life; they all take a complete back seat to your progeny, - or at least they probably should.

Why should a person give up the rest of their life for a child that they don't want, based solely on the ideology of another person's religious based convictions?

Ultimately, this is what it boils down to, isn't it, Roberta? If humanity possessed any proof that a fetus was anything more than a clump of rapidly dividing cells, albeit human, with no more than the *potential* to become a productive member of society, we would never allow abortion. We allow abortion because there is no evidence to suggest that a fetus is anything more than potential.

It is religion that has invented a soul and placed it within each of us at the moment of conception, not some benign or omnipotent overlord. This is your belief, it is not evidence based. You have formed an opinion based on *your* interpretation of *your* doctrine. This is precisely the reason that secularism is so important; it keeps religious ideologies and doctrines the hell away from policy and legislation.

With this in mind, over one third of all pregnancies self terminate within the first three months of conception.

For reasons ranging from a temperature imbalance, to hormones, to something else entirely, one in three pregnancies will be rejected and expelled. Some of these self-terminating pregnancies can occur within days, others months. For all intents and purposes, you could perform a qualitative Beta-Human Chorionic Gonadotrophin (B-HCG) blood test on them a couple days after conception and the hormones would show a pregnancy. As a non-believer, I know that this means that the 'conditions' simply weren't conducive for a full term pregnancy, but for a believer, this explanation should not be acceptable. For a believer, the explanation should be obvious, God said no and terminated the pregnancy Himself! What a prick! God is obviously pro-choice.

You so called 'Pro-Lifer's' are so outwardly concerned with preserving the life of these clumps of cells, but don't give a second's thought to the thousands of ants, flies and mosquitoes you'll crush in your lifetime. What about the thousands of livestock that will die for your sustenance, or the infinite number of bacterium that you'll kill with anti-biotic medication in your lifetime, or the trees used to build your houses?

All of those animals, bacterium, trees and insects are alive in the same way that a fetus is alive, and yet you couldn't give a toss what happens to them, could you? So, get your head out of your collective corpulent asses and stop referring to yourself as 'pro-life'. You are, anti-abortion!

What about the children born to parents that don't want them, what about them? Born into poverty, with little hope of being adequately provided for, with little access to education. What about them? How many children have you adopted this year, Roberta?

The unborn, as you say, are 'alive', but only in the way that a blood clot or a colony of E. coli is alive. A fetus is a clump of cells, nothing more. It is the anti-abortionist chums have given a fetus more meaning than nature actually provides.

While I don't necessarily advocate abortion, I am completely cognizant of the incredible personal growth that all must make prior to having a child. If a person is not ready to give that child everything that they deserve, it is best to terminate and try again later (if that's what they want), when they *are* ready. But the choice is theirs alone to make, not yours, Roberta.

I am pro-life, but also pro-choice.

Conserving The US Constitution and Gay Marriage
I love that you have such an ideological view about the use of the US Constitution, and yet at the same time, can only see it from a Christian perspective. This is typical of many Christians... and all Republicans/Conservatives/Tea-Party-ists... And fascists!

Do you realize that the US constitution does not mention "God" once? In fact, the first mention of religion is:

> *"No religious Test shall ever be required as a Qualification to any Office or public Trust under the United States."*

The quote above from Article 6 of The Constitution and the 1st Amendment serve to separate religion from government all together. This should be no surprise considering that the original American settlers founded their new land in an attempt to escape 'religious persecution'… and so they could marry their attractive cousins and found McDonalds, Fanny May, Freddy Mac and GM, and Krispy Kreme and Taco Bell… mmm Krispy Kreme and Taco Bell.

Furthermore, the words "In God We Trust" weren't printed on American coins until 1863 after a religious surge during the Civil War. The phrase wasn't added to paper money until 1957. The words, "One Nation Under God" isn't in the original Pledge of Allegiance either:

> *"I pledge allegiance to the Flag of the United States of America and to the Republic for which it stands, one nation, indivisible, with liberty and justice for all."*

"One Nation Under God" wasn't in the pledge until 1954 when it was added by congress. Snooty bastards! To top this, many of the founding fathers were both publicly and proudly either deist (educated belief in a universal order; like agnosticism for the wealthy and educated) or atheist. This included Thomas Jefferson, Benjamin Franklin, James Madison, John Adams, Thomas Paine and even George Washington.

Again, America was founded in the name of individuals seeking respite from religious imposition, so it is hard to believe that anyone descended from these people would seek to impose religion on others... or are you calling America religiously hypocritical? That's not patriotic at all! You need to call Faux News (pronounced "Fox News") right now and get yourself an "American Patriot" hat… say 'hi' to Bill-O for me!

You say, Roberta, that you're against judges and legislators who create legislation based on their own ideologies, but this is exactly what legislation banning abortion is, it is exactly what creationist legislators are doing, it is exactly what opponents to legalizing euthanasia and gay marriage are doing! These legislators are imposing their own beliefs and ideologies on the public. Regardless of how many Americans share or refute that ideology, it is a religious based belief, and as such it is wrong to impose it.

While it should not be a big surprise to any atheist who has visited the following states, did you know that Texas, Arkansas, Mississippi, Maryland, Tennessee, North and South Carolina all have an article in their state constitution which stipulates that no atheist can hold a position in politics within the state? South Carolina's constitution states:

"Disqualifications for Office First; any person who shall deny the existence of the almighty God."

This is sad and sorry stuff, Roberta; this goes to show that the people in these states put the requirement for belief in God before, say, the requirement for an above average intelligence.

So you can monitor all of the judicial nominations you want, but if you criticize a single one of their decisions based on your biblical ideologies, recognize that you are being nothing more than another stinking Christian hypocrite!

You say that, "we will be happy to support nominees that abide by a philosophy of applying the original understanding of our Constitution," but these nominees would be the ones supporting wholly secular legislation. The Founding Fathers were smart dudes, Roberta; they wanted a complete separation of Church ideology and State legislature. Basically, you're saying that you want secular legislators. I'm totally ok with this!

From a secular perspective:

- there would be no problem with same sex marriage
- gender or sexuality would be irrelevant in cases of adoption where the prospective parents are otherwise ideal
- sexuality or religious belief would be irrelevant to qualification for military or governmental appointments
- abortion serves a greater good for the individual
- abortion of unwanted pregnancies may alleviate a long term burden on the health and welfare system by making a small once off investment
- there would be no problem with voluntary euthanasia
- a person should have a the right to die with dignity
- no person should be discriminated against, under any circumstances, for any reason, ever

This is what you said you wanted, Roberta.

The Sanctity of Marriage

The traditional definition of marriage in Christianity is male malevolent domination over female subservience. Don't kid yourself:

"Wives must not disrupt worship, talking when they should be listening, asking questions that could more appropriately be asked of their husbands at home. God's Book of the law guides our manners and customs here. Wives have no license to use the time of worship for unwarranted speaking. Do you – both women and men – imagine that you're a sacred oracle determining what's right and wrong? Do you think everything revolves around you?" (1 Corinthians 14:33-39 NIV)

"And every woman who prays or prophesies with her head uncovered dishonors her head – it is just as though her head were shaved." (1 Corinthians 11:5 NIV)

"A woman should learn in quietness and full submission." (Timothy 2:11 NIV)

Get the point, Roberta?

Marriage, for thousands of years, has been used to enslave women. After these thousands of years, it was the women in society who eventually spoke out and changed their role in society for the better. As a consequence of the feminist movement, women who were previously forced into submission and servitude are now able to be all they want to be, in every way.

So if the role of women in marriage has changed, completely and totally (and some time ago), doesn't that mean that marriage has already been irrefutably redefined?

Roberta, how many goats or head of cattle were given to your parents as dowry when you were to be married? Do I hear "none"? Well, that is because the traditional ideal of marriage has already been radically redefined! As such, do you maybe think that it's time to dismount your sanctimonious high-horse and accept that the tradition of marriage has changed because the ideology of society has changed.

Look, Roberta, even up to 50 years ago, women just like you, would have had no right to speak up about politics, much less complain about it! In fact, if you expressed an opinion about politics to your husband or father, he would have laughed at you, patted you on the butt and told you to get back in the kitchen, where it belonged... oh, and get me a beer while you're at it Dear.

Nowadays, we know that this was completely wrong.

Women fought for your right to speak up in a public forum, a right that you didn't have before. Women fought for your right to be whom and what you wanted to be, a right you didn't have before. The rights that those women fought for made sense to an entire generation of women and as a consequence, they got what they wanted, which is what they had always deserved. There are some fairly significant parallels that one can draw between the demand for women's rights and equality the demand for gay, lesbian and transgender rights and equality.

So why do you seek to deny the rights of another minority based on their sexuality? Women were discriminated against for millennia, just for being a less dominant/aggressive sex, now you have acquired the right to not be discriminated against, you're using those rights to discriminate against others, just because their sexual preference is different to yours. Can you smell the hypocrisy?

That old and tired argument you gave, 'that children will become confused when they see same sex parents' is a silly one. Obviously, there will never be as many gay parents as strait ones and in those cases where there are gay parents, you can quite rationally tell children that, "some families have a mommy and a daddy, others have two daddies and others two mommies, and others still have a gorilla and a circus midget". It's not that hard, children aren't confused unless you give them a reason to be confused… for example, say you tell them that an invisible benevolent magical bearded sky-pixie is silently judging everyone for their actions, all of the time, oh, and He also hates the gays!

Nonetheless, the rational world applauds Barak Obama and all other progressives in their quest for equality, and indeed marriage rights for same sex couples (not that Obama will ever allow gay marriage). The Defense of Marriage Act should be repealed; it is defending an ideology that has already been altered irreparably. Gay people deserve love too, Roberta, don't forget that; Gay people deserve love too!

Fairness Doctrine for TV and Radio

With respect to your issues on the Fairness Doctrine, I'm utterly perplexed as to why anyone would ever have any opposition to it. Previously, it was established to ensure broadcasters devote some of their airtime to discussing controversial matters of public interest, and to air contrasting views regarding those matters. So, unless the only channel you watch is Faux News, you shouldn't really have any problem! Welcome to the 'no spin zone', my ass!

Nonetheless, *you* claim that Obama wants to bring back the 'Fairness Doctrine', however, in June 2008, Barack Obama's press secretary wrote that Obama (then a Democratic U.S. Senator from Illinois and candidate for President):

"Does not support reemploying the Fairness Doctrine on broadcasters ... [and] considers this debate to be a distraction from the conversation we should be having about opening up the airwaves and modern communications to as many diverse viewpoints as possible. That is why Sen. Obama supports media-ownership caps, network neutrality, public broadcasting, as well as increasing minority ownership of broadcasting and print outlets."

In February 2009, a White House spokesperson said that President Obama continues to oppose the revival of the Doctrine.

Don't get me wrong, I know that the leader of the Crazy-Brigade Glenn 'everyone-who-isn't-me-is-a-Nazi-Comunist' Beck has been claiming that Obama wanted to bring back the fairness doctrine for a long time now. You need to realize, however, that absolutely nothing that comes out of Beck's mouth is classed as 'viable information'; he is an entertainer and has claimed as much, several times on his show! In fact, I'm not even convinced that the multitudes of deep breaths that he takes for emphasis during his show are real, I think that he is a Nazi-cyborg sent from a future alternate reality where Carl Marx and his fascist wife, who is known only as 'healthcare reform' runs the world. And I need to take a deep breath.

It seems that as long as you wear your heart (Republican pin) on your sleeve (lapel of your Gucci suit jacket) and you're a raving lunatic, Fox will give you your very own "news" show. There, you can propagandize the hell out of just about anything that you're opposed to! In 2010, Sarah Palin joined the Fox News team to give her perspective on just how much the Democrats suck for trying to reform all of the sectors that Bush 'spilled his seed' on.

But seriously, what are you afraid of in the fairness doctrine anyway, Roberta? Are you afraid that someone will do a proper research expose` on Christianity and uncover the fact that biblical-Jesus never really existed and was in fact just and amalgamation of a real life (albeit completely human) apocalyptic preacher and ancient god-in-the-flesh myth?

You are right though, if the fairness doctrine did come back, conservative radio and Christian TV channels might have to educate instead of propagandize and a positive story on any non-conservative-Republican politician might make it to air. I can see it now, just after Pat Robertson gives his, "we're all screwed because of abortion and tolerance of homosexuals in America", Michael Shermer (well known American Skeptic) debunks God... I would watch that show... but it just ain't going to happen.

Stem Cells

Stem cell research is an incredible area of study, Roberta. Diseases and injuries that cripple billions of humans can be halted in their tracks, and damage can possibly even be reversed when stem cell research is applied to clinical practice. Everything from spinal cord injury to motor neurone disease (Prof. Stephen Hawkings' disease) could be virtually eliminated within this or the next generation, providing these fields get the right amount of funding and the right access (if restrictions are removed) to material.

While you say quite rightly that adult stem-cell harvesting for research has had many promising new developments, the problem is, however, harvesting stem cells from adults is *a)* incredibly painful (huge needles that dig into your hip bone), *b)* extremely dangerous (as drugs are required to liberate the stem cells from the bone marrow), *c)* obscenely expensive (drugs, day surgery, patient recovery) and *d)* for very little return (few cells recovered from adults). When you couple all of these things together you are severely and detrimentally affected in the volume, complexity and quality of research you can do on stem cells.

You see, the reason why embryonic stem-cell research is viable is because it is relatively cheap (in comparison to adult harvesting), no pain is felt by anyone or anything and the embryo produces a surplus of stem cells for harvesting. So instead of wasting huge swathes of cash on the harvesting process, the time and money is able to be put into the actual research and applying it to humanity's woes. This obviously makes a humungous difference to the quality and amount of research that can be done and means, possibly, that more cures will come faster.

It probably needs to be recognized, Roberta, that when an embryo is terminated and harvested for stem-cells, it is a maximum of around 5 days post fertilization and consists of around 100-150 cells. To put it into context, your average gram of soil contains around 40 million bacterial cells. To put it into further context, a human adult has around 100 trillion cells. So when we talk about the human embryos used for stem cell research, we're talking about something smaller than the width of a human hair and something that is most assuredly nothing more than a clump of cells in a Petri dish.

Currently, the embryos used for stem cell research all come from surplus embryos from IVF transplantations. This equates to around 70,000 a year in Australia alone. These unused embryos are destined for medical waste bins and will be terminated anyway. So by using them for stem cell research instead of simply tossing them in the bin, they have the potential to save billions of lives in the future.

Ultimately, the embryos never had the potential for life; they were always going to be surplus waste material. So either they're used to cure and heal or they're used as fuel in a medical waste incinerator… who is more naïve now, Roberta?

In fact, maybe we should call your pissy God in to weigh in on this subject:

> "Woe to those who call evil good and good evil, who put darkness for light and light for darkness, who put bitter for sweet and sweet for bitter." (Isaiah 5:20-21 NIV)

Seriously, Roberta, it's not as if there is some sort of evil embryo making factory, impregnating women, then forcing their abortions, churning out fertilized embryos as the factory manager twists his moustache and laughs maniacally. These are unused clumps of cells, which have to be created in order to ensure the efficacy of IVF treatment, which would otherwise be nothing more than medical waste. Any argument against embryonic stem cell research is coming from a position of complete ignorance. These unused clumps of cells will save lives, end suffering – it may even cure blindness (macular degeneration) and allow people to walk again (after spinal cord injury)... stem cells are Jesus 2.0... better yet, we have actual evidence that stem cells are real and work, so they're more like Jesus 1.0 (but real).

Despite your objections, the rational world will continue to work on embryonic stem cell research and create the cures that we so desperately need in order to adequately overpopulate the Earth and completely strip it of all available resources. And when a cure is available for whatever diseases plague you and your family, make sure that you denounce them for the evils that they so clearly are, so that you can live with dignity... and chronic pain and possibly prolonged, drawn out death... but at least a clump of cells destined for a medical waste incinerator wouldn't have been harmed to save your quality of life!

Politics and Taxes for Cretins

With respect to your claims that ex-President George 'Dubya' Bush lowered taxes and Obama is set to raise taxes, I think you need to take a good look at what old Dubya did to the economy and perhaps why Obama will inevitably need to up the taxes. Really, it doesn't matter what country you live in, everyone is going to look favorably on someone who cuts taxes and the dude who ups taxes will be looked on with scorn and contempt and rotten tomatoes to the face!

It firstly needs to be recognized that Bush's so called tax cuts, were tax cuts for people earning over $150,000 per year. While that may well be you, Roberta, it sure as hell isn't the majority of Americans.

In fact, when Obama was debating McCain in the lead-up to the presidential election, every time McCain brought up tax increases, Obama simply said (paraphrasing), "you and I, John, don't need a tax cut; you and I can afford to pay higher taxes. It's the low and middle income earners that need the tax cuts."

It also needs to be recognized that when Bush was president, he royally screwed the economy without so much as a kiss goodnight, or a cab fare home in the morning! He deregulated the bejesus out of the finance sector (without re-bejesusing it before he left, no less); he made sure all his banker buddies were well fed and financed; he started some quasi-religious wars he would never have a chance of finishing - wars that thus far have cost SEVERAL TRILLION DOLLARS; and then he failed to act when people were foreclosing on their houses in droves and the banks developed huge money leaks that they had no chance of plugging!

You speak of bipartisanship, but both sides of US politics were telling Bush to do something about banking and finance regulation and the burgeoning market implosion that was simmering, but good ole Dubya sat by sucking his thumb and praying to Jesus for intercession! The only reason Obama would be required to increase taxes is because the last president completely ruined the American economy.

All throughout this most recent Healthcare Reform debate, we had (mainly) droves of Republicans crying foul over the cost of Healthcare to the American people given the state of debt. Throughout the debate, not a single Republican would acknowledge the part they played putting America in such a state. Wake up and smell the hypocrisy, Roberta!

Christian Privilege in the Military

You claim that evangelical Christian military chaplains and other personnel are being discriminated against 'as they have been during the past number of decades', but exactly when and where have these events taken place? The only reports of religious discrimination in the military were related to Christians assaulting, defaming and discriminating against atheists and agnostics, and this is rampant in the military.

The old saying, "there are no atheists in fox holes" is constantly being tossed around by top military brass in an effort to discredit atheists and agnostics. Recently, Lt. Gen. H. Steven Blum made controversial remarks about atheist and agnostic soldiers while addressing an NAACP convention. Blum said "Agnostics, atheists and bigots suddenly lose all that when their life is on the line....Something that they lived their whole life believing gets thrown out the door, and they grasp the comrade next to them, and they don't care what color their skin is, and they don't care when they pray".

Now, while I'll leave the grouping of bigots and atheists/agnostics alone for now, the sentiment is clear, there is no respect for atheists in the military. When formal complaints and Equal Opportunity claims were raised against Blum for his divisive and blatantly ignorant statements, the response from his department was: "since atheism is not a religion, atheists are not protected by the regulation and it is acceptable for officers and chaplains to disparage their own soldiers". Nice.

On April 26, 2004, Pat Tillman, who had given up an NFL career as Safety for the Arizona Cardinals to fight for his country, had been killed due to friendly fire (a most blatant oxymoron) while engaging the enemy in south-eastern Afghanistan. Tillman sacrificed a lot to do what he thought was right, and because of this, the White House spun the story - into a legendary heroic tale of an all American boy, sacrificing all to fight for his country - so as to solicit public support for the war effort.

John McCain and some other politicians attended his funeral and gave epithets praising god for people like Pat Tillman... pity Tillman was an atheist! Luckily though, Tillman's brother, Richard stood up and said:

> *"He (Pat) would want me to say this. He's not with God. He's f*cking dead. He's not religious. So thanks for your thoughts. But he's bloody dead."*

In an interview on *Real Time with Bill Maher*, Richard added:

> *"I found it (their eulogies) offensive. It's like, I don't go to a church and say, 'This is bullshit,' so don't come to my brother's service and tell me he's with God. He's simply not with f*cking God."*

Sarah Palin, said the following on the 18th of October, 2010:

> *"One of those heroes was from right here in San Jose, who gave up money and the glamour. And think what he sacrificed and his family sacrificed, giving up a pro-football career to serve his country and ultimately giving up his life for our freedom. Remember to thank God every day for Pat and for the thousands like him..."*

What Palin didn't say was that Tillman had been bullied for his atheism and the disdain he held towards the Iraq and Afghanistan conflicts. What Palin didn't say was that he had been shot in suspicious circumstances, from within 10 feet. No formal inquest has been lodged despite the military medical examiners finding that were suspicions about the close proximity of the three bullets.

While it is obviously true that atheism is not a religion, if one engages in disparagement or ridicule directed towards an atheist, based on the fact that the person is an atheist whilst they are Christian, they are effectively doing so on the basis of religious belief. It's like saying that you can't discriminate against blacks, but its fine to discriminate on the basis that someone is 'not white' or it being fine to discriminate against men who don't like vagina's or women who like vagina's too much. It is unacceptable and perfectly illustrates a systemic lack of respect for those without belief in the supernatural in the military.

Based on this, it is utterly ridiculous to suggest that any Christian in the military is being discriminated against because they are Christian (if anything, it's the exact opposite). This simply demonstrates your ignorance towards those who identify as being atheists.

Christians are so quick to play the persecution card; they're like the soccer players of the religious world. You can have a Christian berating you, harassing you, calling 'what you do' and 'how you act' and 'how you speak' deplorable (and I've had this happen far too many times), and then the second you turn around and begin intellectually refuting their claims, they shove their fingers in their ears, close their eyes and shout "QUIT PERSECUTING ME!" Poor little buggers! They're perfectly adept at distributing criticisms, but they are completely unable to handle any themselves.

It is absolutely brilliant that military chaplains are now forbidden from praying during military functions, but this does not, in any way, shape or form, constitute discrimination. In fact, it is the antithesis of discrimination. It is showing great tolerance for all who are not Christian; it shows equality, restraint and consideration. All that religion does is segregate; it immediately creates a barrier of 'us and them', and in the military, this cannot be allowed to perpetuate.

'Praying in the name of Jesus', as you put it, discriminates against agnostics, atheists, Muslims, Buddhists, Jews, Hindus, and any other religion that does not acknowledge JC as anything more than an angry, uppity Jew who died 2000 years ago in protest of the very institutions Christianity created in his name. These are people too! They have every right to their beliefs or lack thereof! They have every right to fight and die for their country and little piss-ants like you, Roberta, without having the belief in a magical sky-pixie imposed on them. You, just like Bush, need to realize that military service is not service for Jesus. It is service for Country.

Our old mate Bush considered the war on terror in Iraq and Afghanistan to be the same as the holy wars of medieval times. Bush warned Americans that:

> *"This crusade, this war on terrorism, is going to take awhile." (George Bush, September 19, 2001)*

Bush remarked, throughout his presidency, that everyone has the right to worship or believe in which ever god they wished, or no god at all. In the grand scheme of things, that is a positive step over Bush Senior's assertion that atheists weren't actual citizens.

That said, Junior either didn't understand or at least didn't believe in the constitutionally mandated separation of church and state. He regularly promoted HIS religion with faith-based programs run by proponents of HIS religion and openly governed according to HIS religious ideals, beliefs and delusions.

"[Jesus said] He that is not with me is against me."
(Matthew 12:30 NIV)

This stupid belief that 'if you're not Christian, then you're anti-America, anti-patriot and a fascist, Nazi, communist,' is beyond a joke. 200+ years of allowing military chaplains to pray in the name of Jesus and according to their faith requirements is tired, old nonsense. The fact that something is 'traditional' does not immediately make it right! Slavery continued for millennia because it was traditional to do so; the oppression of Blacks and women has endured for millennia because it was traditional to do so; witch doctors, shamans and faith healers did nothing for anyone, ever, and yet in the absence of actual medicine, parents have sent sick children to them for millennia; husbands have beaten their wives, for doing little more than questioning them, for millennia, should they continue to do so for the sake of tradition?

Tradition for traditions stake is a copout to humanity. We grow, we advance and we develop. We learn from our previous generation's successes and failures and advance ourselves for the better, and hope that our children will do the same. It seems that all Christianity is good for is holding humanity back. Silencing and discrediting scientists for advancing our understanding of the universe, is that all you're good for? Converting or killing those who think differently or have different opinions on the same God (Jews and Muslims), is that all you're good for? Discriminating against or persecuting those without beliefs, is that all you're good for?

Ultimately you make the most compelling case possible for complete disbelief. All of the policies you say you will fight for either discriminate against or disadvantage one or more groups of people. Same sex marriage, those who want or need abortions, those who want an end to conservative propaganda on TV, those who stand to benefit from embryonic stem cell research, those who like high taxes, and every non-Christian in the military, you bag them all for your own ideological ends.

Christianity isn't about love, tolerance and togetherness, it's about hate, intolerance and segregation. Sure you love and want to congregate around those that think, talk, act and enjoy the smell of their own rectal discharge as you do, but if you don't fit within that little box, you're an enemy of Jesus Christ!

For God's sake, start doing what the Apostle Paul told you to do and shut the hell up!

Personally, I hate zombies, so I'm cool with being an enemy of Jesus; shit, call me anti-Christ if you like!

Peace out.

Jake Farr-Wharton

Why Does God Allow Evil?

Rick Warren is the founding pastor of Saddleback Church in Lake Forest, Calif., one of America's largest and best-known churches. In addition, Rick is author of the New York Times best seller *The Purpose Driven Life* and *The Purpose Driven Church*, which was named one of the 100 Christian books that changed the 20th century. He is also founder of Pastors.com, a global Internet community for ministers.

The horrific mass murder of innocent Americans leaves all rational people shocked, angry, grief-stricken and numb. Our tears flow freely and our hearts carry a deep ache. How could this happen in our nation?

As mothers, fathers, brothers, sisters, friends, neighbors and coworkers begin to share their stories of the horror, this tragedy will become even more personal. As it becomes more personal, it will become more painful, and as our pain deepens, so will the questions. Why does God allow evil to happen? If God is so great and so good, why does he allow human beings to hurt each other?

The answer lies in both our greatest blessing and our worst curse: our capacity to make choices. God has given us a free will. Made in God's image, he has given us the freedom to decide how we will act and the ability to make moral choices. This is one asset that sets us apart from animals, but it also is the source of so much pain in our world. People, and that includes all of us, often make selfish, self-centered and evil choices. Whenever that happens, people get hurt.

Sin is ultimately selfishness. I want to do what I want, not what God tells me to do. Unfortunately, sin always hurts others, not just ourselves.

God could have eliminated all evil from our world by simply removing our ability to choose it. He could have made us puppets, or marionettes on strings that he pulls. By taking away our ability to choose it, evil would vanish. But God doesn't want us to be puppets. He wants to be loved and obeyed by creatures who voluntarily choose to do so. Love is not genuine if there is no other option.

Yes, God could have kept the terrorists from completing their suicidal missions by removing their ability to choose their own will instead of his. But to be fair, God also would have to do that to all of us. You and I are not terrorists, but we do harm and hurt others with our own selfish decisions and actions.

You may hear misguided minds say, "This must have been God's will." Nonsense!

In a world of free choices, God's will is rarely done! Doing our own will is much more common. Don't blame God for this tragedy. Blame people who ignored what God has told us to do: "Love your neighbor as yourself."

In Heaven, God's will is done perfectly. That's why there is no sorrow, pain or evil there. But this is Earth, a fallen, imperfect place. We must choose to do God's will everyday. It isn't automatic. This is why Jesus told us to pray, "Thy will be done on earth, as it is in Heaven."

The Bible explains the root of evil: "This is the crisis we're in: God's light streamed into the world, but men and women everywhere ran for the darkness ... because they were not really interested in pleasing God" (John 3:19, Message Translation). We're far more interested in pleasing ourselves.

There are many other questions that race through our minds during dark days. But the answers will not come from pollsters, pundits or politicians. We must look to God and his Word. We must humble ourselves and admit that each of us often choose to ignore what God wants us to do.

No doubt houses of worship across America will be packed in the coming days. In a crisis we cry out for a connection with our Creator. This is a deep-seated, universal urge. The first words uttered by millions on Sept. 11 were "Oh God!"

We were made for a relationship with God, but he waits for us to choose him. He is ready to comfort, guide and direct us through our grief. But it's your choice.

Dear Rick,

I appreciate your efforts to provide solace to those who tragically lost loved ones on 9/11, but what I don't care for is your misguided, self-delusional, and erroneous rationale. In other words, you display a level of 'douche-baggery' that, I dare say, will be tough to top. And I feel it important to lay my cards on the table, so to speak, for fear you will mistakenly believe there be hidden passive-aggression throughout the remainder of this letter. That is not the case, Rick, not at all.

I really enjoyed your brilliant deduction that God permitted jetliners to be flown as building seeking missiles. It suggests that not only did God provide the nineteen hijackers the necessary free will to carry out their dastardly deeds, but also more curiously, you imply that all of those involved in 9/11 were made in his very image, your words.

Free Will and Ghosts
Well, first of all Rick, if the Hamburg franchise of Al-Qaeda were truly made in God's image, then quite clearly they'd be invisible, incorporeal and for all intents and purposes, non-existent. Or is that your point? Are you suggesting they were able sneak past security scanners at Boston's Logan International Airport because they were able to switch to 'holy spirit mode',

i.e. as a ghost, and slip through? Otherwise, your point makes as much sense as wanting to join the 'mile-high-club' in the bathroom of the economy section in the later stages of a long haul Air India flight immediately after the combination meat curry has been served. Just trust me on that, ok?

Your letter invokes a number of questions, so put down the donut, you corpulent crusader of Christos, and pay attention! Can you explain to the readers, how it is free will, if God decrees it to you? Objectively, you are implying that God made a decision not to impose his power over our respective choices. But this doesn't make any sense against your Christian faith.

What does the New Testament tell us about free will? It says that I am free to do whatever I choose but below this fine proclamation there is the fine print; a caveat regarding eternal salvation. The terms and conditions of my free will decree that I accept that a Jew by the name of Jesus of Nazareth was tortured to death in a savagely grotesque manner somewhere in Palestine 2000 years ago and in doing so, saved my soul… well, saved my soul if I accept him as my 'personal lord and savior'.

If I refuse to accept said testimony, then I am tortured for eternity in the burning infernos of Hell.

Hardly sounds like a genuine offer of free choice, does it?

This is the fundamental belief of the Christian faith, the dogmatic ideology that you employ to indoctrinate your fellow human beings from early childhood. Or have I got it wrong? Is it *totally* evidence based and I'd just missed out on the dossier?

The whole, "this world was made for you, do with it as you please… but remember that the fires of Hell await if you do, say or think anything contrary to our... I mean God's decree" - is this the free will you refer to? Hardly free if it costs you all the enjoyment and experience that life has to offer, is it?

Further complicating the whole 'free will' claim is that the Bible states the exact opposite. Open your Good Book and thumb your way to Ecclesiastes 7, Ephesians 1, Ephesians 2, Acts 13, Romans 8, Romans 9, 2 Timothy, 2 Thessalonians, and Revelations. Passages that clearly show that God's unending and constantly changing plans (God has terrible mood swings, you see; like a perpetual teenager) override our free will.

In fact, the Bible makes frequent assertions that God creates and directly intervenes in our future and accordingly decides our fate, regardless of what our own will is. I am not making this stuff up, Ricky, my boy! Not only have I directed you to the relevant scriptures but you mustn't forget that the principles of pre-destination (that God mysteriously engenders everything) was taught by the founding fathers of Western Christianity, including St. Augustine, Martin Luther, and John Calvin.

Still not satisfied? Then I quote God's book for you:

> *"But because of his great love for us, God, who is rich in mercy, made us alive with Christ even when we were dead in transgressions – it is by grace you have been saved. And God raised us up with Christ and seated us with him in the Heavenly realms in Christ Jesus, in order that in the coming ages he might show the incomparable riches of his grace, expressed in his kindness to us in Christ Jesus. For it is by grace you have been saved, through faith – **and this not from***

yourselves, it is the gift of God – not by works, so
that no one can boast. For we are God's workmanship,
created in Christ Jesus to do good works, **which God
prepared in advance for us to do**." *(Ephesians 2:4-10)*

The 9/11 Terrorists Were Doing God's Work...
Just Like You!

Rick, are you aware the 9/11 attacks were committed by
deeply devout, pious and religious men (just like Jesus
or your fine self) who worship the same god as you (the
God of Abraham)? Or, do you share in the typically
Conservative/Evangelical/Below-Average-
IQ/Republican view that the perpetrators of 9/11 were
just a rag tag bunch of evildoers? Judging by your
article, and just about every word that escapes your
mouth, it would suggest the later.

Now, I'm sure you really don't want to hear this, but the
actions of Mohammed and his gang of 40 terrorists
really, truly, deeply, passionately, warmly, sincerely
pleased and aroused Abraham's God and Jesus' daddy.
Nothing gets God aroused like seeing his follower's
murder individuals and societies that do not obey his
law (the correct law, not the one those other people
worship) to the highest degree. If you aren't stabbing,
murdering, exploding, hijacking, hand-grenading and
terrorizing in God's name... you're not a real believer!
Hell, you aren't even a real man!

As a matter of fact, God is pissed by your mambly-
pambly pacifism, and no doubt thinks you're a bit of a
pussy. Radical/extremist Islam has the same opinion.
God even spells out his ethnic cleansing bloodlust in
'capitals' as will I:

"If you hear it said about one of the towns the Lord your God is giving you to live in that wicked men have arisen among you and have led the people astray, saying, 'Let us go and worship other gods', then you must enquire, probe and investigate it thoroughly. And if it is true and it has been proved that this detestable thing has been done among you, you must certainly put the sword to all who live in that town. Destroy it completely, both its people and its livestock. Gather all the plunder of the town into the middle of the town square and completely burn the town and all its plunder as a whole burnt offering to the Lord your God." (Deuteronomy 13:12-16)

Not only does he command you to murder non-believers but also he demands that you dance around the bon-fire fueled by their belongings and skulls. This is, in effect, what the hijackers did. I guess we can clearly say that Al-Qaeda, in that regard, are men of perfect and resolute faith. Yeah, yeah I know they read the Koran, and not the Bible, but it's the same God, the God of Abraham... it's just written by *another* desert nomad with a blood lust. God, in his Arabic addendum, the Koran, words it a little more subtlety but the message is not lost:

"Slay them wherever you find them. Drive them out of the places from which they drove you. Idolatry is worse than carnage. If they attack you put them to the sword. Thus shall the unbelievers be rewarded: but if they desist, God is forgiving and merciful. Fight against them until idolatry is no more and God's religion reigns supreme. But if they desist, fight none except the evildoers." (Koran: 2:190-93)

So get off your buttocks, Rick and go slay some Buddhist extremists; it will help God with his erectile dysfunction problems. Remember what Jesus said:

> "[Jesus said] He who is not with Me is against Me, and he who does not gather with Me scatters." (Luke 11:23)

Clones, Not Puppets

"But God doesn't want us to be puppets. He wants to be loved and obeyed by creatures who voluntarily choose to do so," you say. Really? So you're saying that God is happy if we voluntarily choose not to worship him? Oh that's sweet. I like that. That's a nice god. Ok, I won't doubt you, but I'm just going to cross reference that with what it says in the Bible. God says to Moses in Deuteronomy:

> "If your very own brother, or your son or daughter, or the wife you love, or your closest friend secretly entices you, saying, 'Let's go out and worship other gods', do not yield to him or listen to him. Show him no pity. Do not spare him or shield him. You must certainly put him to death. Your hand must be the first in putting him to death, and then the hands of the people. Stone him to death because he tried to turn you away from the Lord your God…..Then all Israel will hear and be afraid, and no-one among you will do such an evil thing again." (Deuteronomy 13:6-11)

HOLY SHIT, you deceptive bastard, you duped me again! Voluntarily obey him? Hmm are we talking about the same God here? Or are you referring to the big fat, smiling, happy looking Chinese guy again? Because this god, your god, demands that I murder my own daughter if I catch her worshipping the Wiggles... or worse... one of the Jonas Brothers. Also, I think your definition of volunteering is the same as the Taliban Recruitment Director in Pushtan Province. His slogan is "You fight great American Satan or we behead your youngest child before your very own eyes... but it's *totally* your choice." Sound familiar?

What I find staggering is that you are regarded as *America's* Pastor, but either you're willfully ignorant of the Biblical context and historicity, or you are deceitfully manipulative of the text that forms the underlining of your own messages. Which one is it? Case in point, you quote Jesus' "Love your neighbor", but then you conveniently leave off the sub-text, that being Jesus, and the Old Testament meant "Love your neighbor, but ONLY if he's Hebrew." God hates anyone that's not a Hebrew. Heck, he even commanded Joshua to slaughter all non-Jews the Israelites encountered along the path to the Promised Land.

When Jesus said, "Love your neighbor", he literally meant the dude in the tent next to you. The people in the next valley and the roaming travelers were to be slaughtered, raped, tortured, raped some more and then slaughtered... then eat the animals... after raping and slaughtering them.

Now, I understand that Apostle Paul did a great job in making Jesus all non-Jewy or at the very least, Judaism-Lite* (or maybe 98% Jew Free), but Jesus was most assuredly a devout, Orthodox, Moses loving, circumcised Jew. He was a proud Jew who fully endorsed all terms and conditions of the Hebrew tradition, namely Mosaic law.

There's even that lovely scene in the Book of Matthew that has a Canaanite woman pleading with Jesus to heal her demonically possessed daughter. Jesus refuses. She begs some more. Jesus tells her that his magic caresses are reserved for Jews only, "I am sent only for the lost sheep of Israel". She cries and pleads some more. Jesus tells her to get lost. In fact he uses stronger language than that:

> "[Jesus says] It is not right to take the children's bread and toss it to their dogs." (Matthew 21:26 NIV)

Yes, he called her a dog, which was as low an insult anyone could make at an obvious low point in her life. Sweet Jesus, huh? Yeah, sweet as arsenic flavored candy plucked from the ass-cheeks of an obese geriatric!

You Is Eeeevil

This whole evil business must give you sleepless nights. He's evil! They're evil. Those believers are evildoers. Evil, evil, evil. If you say it enough times then I'm sure it helps in converting frightened little children into God's frightened little children and then plunking them into your church pews. And, hey if they happen to feel compelled to leave a donation, America will be a better place, right?

Fluffy White Clouds, and Mansions For All

"In Heaven," you opined, "God's will is done perfectly. That's why there is no sorrow, pain or evil there." It kind of sounds like you have *actually* been to Heaven. I don't need you to go into much descriptive detail on the ambience up there, but would you mind pointing to where it is on this cool map of the universe I got from

Popular Science Magazine? I have a feeling it's on a big yacht appropriately named "This is Heaven", berthed somewhere in the Maldives... but hey, that's just speculation.

You also mustn't forget that your description of Heaven is in stark contrast to the acid trip described in Revelations. You didn't mention any of the creepy giant beasts with twenty heads, eighty eyes, seventeen penises and a partridge in a pair tree. So where did you get your info on heaven from, because it doesn't seem to match up with the only testimony God provided for humanity?

Which brings me to this question; if there is no sorrow in Heaven, as you proclaim, does this mean all of Heaven's residents feel no anguish for their loved ones that didn't qualify for entrance due to their ambivalence or disbelief? Surely there must be at least one parent upset that their eldest daughter who dabbled in Wicca (Christine O'Donnell) is taking the pointy end of a pineapple up the pooper, every second, of everyday, for a trillion years, multiplied by a trillion years, plus two years, times one hundred trillion years, plus infinity times eternity?

Furthermore, why would an all-loving, all-powerful God permit evil just because he gave us the "gift of free will"? This seems absurd to me. Why doesn't he care that his children suffer... much less, for all eternity? As I parent, I freak out when my children twists their ankle on the jungle gym at the local park, but you and your like-minded brethren imply that God doesn't give a shit because we owe him something in return for his 'gift' to us? It doesn't make a great deal of sense to me, and whilst I may never be a rocket-surgeon, smarter men than I have found equal trouble with your wicked and painfully malevolent conundrum.

Take Epicurus for example, he opined the following riddle three centuries prior to the arrival of your man, Jesus:

> *"Either God wants to abolish evil, and cannot; or he*
> *can, but does not want to. If he wants to, but cannot, he*
> *is impotent. If he can, but does not want to, he is*
> *wicked. If God can abolish evil, and God really wants to*
> *do it, why is there evil in the world?"*

He's got you there, right? Either God is all-powerful or all loving; but he cannot be both. So I ask you, if God is all-powerful and all loving, from where does evil come? Moreover, the free will you speak of hardly comes free of charge does it? It comes wrapped in a parcel of Hell. Your definition of free will is that God gives one the right to choose anything one wants to, whenever one wishes… as long as they believe that God raped a woman in order to give birth to himself, or they'll will burn in Hell for eternity. Again, that's hardly a 'free' offer is it?

You claim that the Bible explains the root of evil as pleasing ourselves over pleasing God, but you've ignorantly (I refuse to consider you as simply naïve) and dangerously forgotten who those men were. Those bastard terrorists who flew those planes into the Twin Towers and the Pentagon, they were men of God. They were pious. They were doing exactly what their manipulative Imams had told them God wanted them to do.

Sam Harris sums up the whole 'loving God and Islam' thing succinctly *in End of Faith*:

"The men who committed the atrocities of September 11 were certainly not "cowards," as they were repeatedly described in the Western media, nor were they lunatics in any ordinary sense. They were men of faith – perfect faith, as it turns out – and this, it must finally be acknowledged, is a terrible thing to be."

While I'm sure that this revelation is hard to accept, it is one that you'll eventually need to recognize. On the 12th of October, 2001, I received a call from my friend who was on a surfing holiday in Bali, Indonesia. He'd walked out of the Sari Club, a popular club for Westerners in the Kuta tourist district, with a serious craving for McDonalds just before midnight. About 15-20 minutes later, Muslim extremists detonated explosives (suicide-bombing terrorists) outside of two of the more popular clubs killing 202 people, including 88 Australians and 38 Indonesian citizens.

These terrorists were, in their own way, pleasing God. Regardless of what you say and regardless of how many biblical verses you quote, you cannot take their piety and commitment to God away from them. Their devotion to God made them who they were, made them do what they did, leading them to completely contravene the human imperative for self-preservation.

By their standards, and indeed by yours, they were moral people acting on behalf of God. Never forget that!

In Case of a Terrorist Attack, Run To Your Nearest Church

You infer that the answers for the questions that arose as a consequence of the 9/11 attacks will not come from anyone but God. Firstly Rick, I have a fundamental problem with this assertion, and I realize you're not the only culprit; but God hasn't done or said anything since impregnating a random virgin in the Middle East 2000 years ago. The prayers of multitudes go unceremoniously unanswered, believers are killed, non-believers are saved; God provides no advice, no guidance, no wisdom or forbearance. The only thing that God provides is a distinct absence.

Even if one were gullible enough to believe the occasions in the Old Testament where God directly intervened in the affairs of the ancient Hebrews to deliver them into the Promised Land (again and again and again and again...) he's done bugger all since. As such, it would be literally insane to humble one's self in admittance that we 'ignore what God wants us to do', because God requires the lips of fallible, often downright morally repugnant preachers to deliver messages that he is apparently not powerful enough to provide Himself.

As you say, plenty of people turned to churches after the attacks on 9/11, but when they asked, "how could God allow this to happen", they were met with a barrage of cliché jibes from biblical history. It *is* humanity's fault, isn't it, Rick? It was wide spread disbelief in God that did it; it was our disobedience and debauchery; our acts of ravenous gluttony and abhorrence. The church has no answers because the church speaks for God and God has no voice, just a set of wooden pews and a collection plate filled with five-dollar bills.

Yeah, the choice is clear; believe or be tortured. Plenty of choice there, pal. Personally, I think I'd prefer Hell; after all, that's where all of the intelligent, fun and interesting people are going! The last thing I'd ever want is to hang out with the lame-ass non-drinking game Morons – crap, sorry, I *totally* meant Mormons - for the rest of eternity!

Anyway, there's a few things for you to chew on, not that you look like a guy that is short of things to chew on. Remember, if God doesn't heal amputees, he sure as hell ain't going to magic away that adipose clogging up your arteries! Just ask Oprah! Shit, now I'm being rude, see what you did?

I just want to leave you with this final thought: The Twin Towers would be standing proudly over Manhattan today, and an additional 3,500 New Yorkers would be returning home for dinner tonight if there was no religion. Sure, that's not the only reason the terrorists were directed to do what they did on 9/11, but you must not ever forget that those terrorists were doing their darndest to please God, your god.

Warm regards,

Jake Farr-Wharton

TO RICK WARREN

Jesus Loves You

Dear Reader, the following is an article by Christian Fundamentalist, Kirk Cameron. Kirk is a former childhood actor, former (self proclaimed) 'atheist and evolutionist', and is currently an evangelical Christian preacher, alongside Ray Comfort, with Living Waters.

He travels America preaching the good word about how everyone who is not an evangelical Christian is going to hell. He also starred in the Christian rapture series, Left Behind. His full address can be found here: *www.livingwaters.com/index.php?option=com_k2&view=ite m&id=821:im-going-back-to-ucla&Itemid=143&lang=en*

I was recently on the UCLA campus, sharing the gospel with students during their lunch break. UCLA is home to some of the most talented and intelligent young people in our country. As we struck up conversations about morality and faith, I quickly realized that for the most part, our young generation of students, soon to be the future business leaders, mothers and fathers, and politicians of our country are operating in a spiritually dead zone. Their minds have been horribly tweaked by the atheist's fairy tale of evolution and post-modern secular brainwashing. It so reminded me of when I was in school, learning about 'science', the history of the universe, geology, astronomy, etc. These kids sounded so intelligent, so self-assured, and so knowledgeable, while at the same time reveling in their idolatry, fornication, deceit, theft, and blasphemy without the slightest concern of eternal consequences. They mocked and laughed at Christ, our God, His Word, and His warnings. They scoffed at the message of the cross and rejected the love of the Savior who bled to save them.

At one point, when discussing the existence of God, one girl told me that she was very afraid of death. She also told me she doesn't believe in God because science has 'proven' that the universe might have been formed without a Creator. She wouldn't budge. The sad thing was that she looked as though she had tears of her heart rebelling against the pride of her intellect, fighting to push their way out her eyes as she insisted that there was no God, no afterlife, and no meaning to her existence. It was as though she didn't want her statements to be true, but was convinced by her professors that her life was nothing more than a cosmic accident and had no meaning beyond the here and now. As we spoke about her sin, the penalty of Hell, and the hope of eternal life through faith in Christ, she just couldn't bring herself to open up. She was polite and charming, but stubborn and self-righteous at the same time. My heart broke for her as she walked off to her next class, attempting to live out the remainder of her days trying to find peace and pleasure before the hand of death steals it all from her.

Another young man I spoke with smirked and laughed at the notion of sin and Judgment Day. He acted as though our conversation was an insult to his intellect. He mocked and scoffed at every turn. He admitted he was liar, a thief, and an adulterer (by the Bible's standards), but said he didn't care. As I pressed God's moral requirements upon his conscience, he finally snapped. He spit out the words, "Then why did God kill my Grandmother?" and "Why does God allow evil?" We had a great discussion about every man's appointed time to die because of sin and God's patience and kindness leading him toward repentance. But in the end, he laughed again, turned and wandered into a crowd of 'super-students' at UCLA, "ever learning, and never able to come to the knowledge of the truth." (2 Timothy 3:7)

I left the campus discouraged and heart-broken, wondering if my evangelistic efforts had any eternal effect on these students. Only God knows, but one thing I have learned: Many of the young people in our world are on their way to Hell and won't believe it until they get there. I can imagine some of them even trying to "scientifically" disprove God as they stand before Him in Judgment, still justifying themselves, while all the witnesses in Heaven, Almighty God, and their own conscience unanimously convict them 'Guilty as Charged'. Perhaps then they will realize that although they 'reasoned' themselves into the world's finest learning institutions, they failed the most important test of eternity. God promises to humble the proud and exalt the humble. Knowledge puffs up and blinds the eyes of the proud. While many of the finest learners have listened well to the teachings of their professors, they have neglected to heed the Word of their Creator, bringing eternal destruction to their own souls.

I'm going back to UCLA next week to talk with some more students. This time, I'm going to speak with much more conviction and urgency. I'm not going to get tied up in intellectual arguments. I won't get discouraged. I'm going to 'do the work of an evangelist' and 'seek and save the lost'.

I'm going to address their greatest need of eternity. I'll appeal to whatever good sense remains in them, use the tools God has given me, and fervently pray for them. These students have their high GPA and SAT scores, but I have the answer to death and the roadmap to Heaven. Please pray for me as I go armed with compassion, hoping to turn some from their sin to the Savior. I will pray for you as you go into your world and do the same.

Dear Kirk,

Let me start by saying, and I'm sure I'm not the first to point this out, that your assertion that the common Cavendish banana is, in fact, the 'atheist nightmare', was by far, the single most hilarious video I had ever seen - probably not for the reasons that you had hoped, though, more so because you clearly and proudly wore your intellect on your sleeve. Good for you, buddy!

I love the fact that you claim to be a 'former evolutionist' yet are clearly unable to tell the difference between a cleverly cultivated, selectively bred and modified fruit that humanity has altered specifically for all of the qualities that you mentioned in your video. Last time I was in the Philippines, I ate a wild banana and I have to tell you man, there is a huge difference between your 'atheist nightmare' and the horrible, bitter, seed filled, hand me a bin I'm going to vomit, fruit that is the wild banana.

Ultimately, all you did was illustrate the lack of understanding Christian evangelicals have of the world that they live in, whilst being ever so excited about their take on it... I think that is commonly referred to as ignorance. But hang in there, sunshine; you're frigging special!

Before I get into addressing your letter, Kirk, I just wanted to define religious belief and faith, because I'll be referring to it, as you did, often; religious belief/faith is; belief *in direct spite* of any and all contrary evidence, faith *in spite* of reason. Clear? Good!

The Dead Zone and Science Brainwashing
I love immensely that what you refer to as a 'spiritually dead zone', the rational and educated world would call 'a place for learning' or 'university'. This next generation of learned individuals will be utterly brilliant, they have, like all before them, an opportunity to learn from, and then supersede their professors.

How dare you presume to know what people require in order to be 'good people'! I find it amazing that you've got such a problem with what you call, 'the atheist's fairy tale of evolution and post-modern secular brainwashing' when what you are actually referring to is a distinct lack of religious brainwashing, or more likely, a refutation of prior religious brainwashing. Think about it, if these students were in your fold; if they were thinking like you think, talking like you talk and waving 'atheist nightmare' bananas in people's faces, you would have no problem with them, in fact, you'd be calling for their election as a State Senator or freaking President! Instead, you denounce them because they have not been brainwashed to think, talk and act without cognitive dissonance as you do. These students aren't 'brainwashed', they're just smart enough to see through this distinct flavor of sanctimonious bullshit.

I find it very interesting that when you refer to the *'science'* that *you* learned, you put it in inverted commas, but when you refer to it later in this article, you've left it without. Is that because the *'science'* you were taught was not actually *'science'*, but in fact some off shoot of 'science'? Perhaps some form of 'pseudo-science' like 'creation science' or (I've heard that 'damn this is good cocaine, I can't feel my teeth' science' is also pretty good science)? Seriously, Kirk, you refer to yourself as a 'former-evolutionist', and yet when you place the *'science'* that you learned in inverted commas, you ultimately display a sincere ignorance towards the field of study that so many Christians also take for granted.

Your car, your shoe, the internet, the sales of your 'Christian mentoring' (I wonder if Catholic priests call it 'Christian mentoring' when they take all those altar boys into their rectories) and 'Way of the Master' programs from your website, your food processing, even your Bible would not be available to you without the 'miracle' of science. See what I did there with the inverted comas?

That said, I shouldn't be surprised that you would place science in inverted comas, after all, you describe yourself as a 'former-evolutionist'. Those of us who actually understand the theorem of biological evolution by way of natural selection find it very hard to believe that one who actually understood it would pack it all up in favor of 'God did it'. What I find more likely is that you had either never actually understood biological evolution, and so, when your limited understanding could not stand up to scrutiny from some charismatic evangelical nut-bag, with a moustache, your 'science' crumbled.

Unlike your Bible, science is something that is *not* and never will be infallible. It is self-correcting and constantly updating itself. A consequence of this, in my experience, is that people like you feel that because you can't understand it or because its conclusions may sometimes change, that it is not worthy of trust. This is ridiculous, science is never a fixed point, it never assumes, presupposes or holds anything sacred. You cannot base your conclusions of science on *your* understanding of science, because your understanding of science is clearly incorrect or at least convoluted by your Evangelical Christian prejudice.

Science, especially that related to the mechanics behind Big Bang theory and biological evolution is not infallible and has never ever claimed to be. Science is not a process of cementing guesses into textbooks, and then preaching said guesses. It is a continual process of reinvention, re-experimentation, revision and renewal. While it is true that Darwin's theory of natural selection has stood the test of time, it is only due to the fact that it is still heavily supported by a wonderful, tangible thing called evidence.

You don't think that Darwin and his contemporaries devised the theory of evolution by way of natural selection by inviting a selection of scientists into a room, then voting on it, do you (i.e. like the First Council of Nicaea)? If and when a new testable, observable, quantitative and/or qualitative theorem is validated which supersedes or disproves natural selection, it will be adopted and the process will continue on.

On the other hand, we have Christianity, Kirk, which remains basically unchanged despite the advances in human intelligence and understanding of the natural laws that govern our existence and universe. Science unashamedly claims fallibility, yet still enriches the lives of humanity to a far greater extent than a book that outlines our most compelling reason for 'being moral' as, "because God punishes you for infinity for finite acts".

Scientists of any field will openly tell you that science is 'great certainty, based on great evidence'; religion on the other hand is certainty in spite of evidence. This doesn't inherently presume that either is 'better' or more correct, after all, no reputable scientist would make the unfounded claim that 'religion is false' or 'there is no such thing as God' without evidence which they do not possess.

The only reason that science is feared and rejected by Christian evangelicals and fundamentalists is because their idea of biblical genesis is directly refuted by biological evolution, cosmology and astronomy, which completely invalidates the premise of their religion.

People fear and reject what they do not understand. It is only natural that people like you, Kirk, would do the same to something that you do not understand. "Zing", implied!

Preaching To The Choir

You went to proselytize at UCLA, Kirk, which is hardly going to be filled with ignoramuses, is it? Obviously, they're going to be intelligent and knowledgeable, you have to be in order to get into a good college, for starters, and then there is the requirement for intelligence that will keep them from flunking. Tied into that is, of course, their self-assurance, as they clearly realize that they are chiefly responsible for their place and grade while studying at UCLA. To me, it sounds like you were intellectually trumped by a bunch of kids who were far more intelligent and knowledgeable that you. But that is just an objective appraisal. Leave the jealousy for God, mate!

Seriously, hearing an overly exuberant evangelical tell an intelligent philosophy major that Jesus loves them and yet wants to see all who don't believe in him burn in Hell forever, to me, is more sickening than watching an obese kid eat a Big Mac.

I hate to be the bearer of bad news, mate, but the fact is that Jesus doesn't love you. In fact, the very fact that you are a gentile (non-Jew) means that he thinks of you as a dog, think Matthew 15:21-28.

Matthew, Mark, Luke and John wrote the only four books of the Bible that testament Jesus' 'life', from then on, anything attributed to Jesus comes in the form of 'visions' and 'dreams'. Mark, who wrote the first

Gospel, didn't even put pen to paper until (at the absolute earliest estimates) 50 years after our old mate was nailed to the cross. Up to that point, the story of Jesus was delivered purely by word of mouth. Chinese whispers, anyone?

Kirk, sex is fun. In fact, sex is bloody fabulous. You were an actor in your teens mate, are you telling the world that you didn't sleep with hundreds of women or men when your acting career was at its height? I thought that's what the life of a young, good looking actor was like! These are students, they're at their prime, they're experimenting with their creativity, their intellect, their understanding of their universe and expanding and exploring their mind; so why not also their bodies? Have you forgotten what it is like to be surrounded by young, hot people of the opposite (or same) sex? They're young and enjoying what life, and their bodies, have to offer... leave the judgment to your God!

Also, what do you mean by 'idolatry'? You say that they're reveling in their 'idolatry', are you referring to the professors who inspire them to do great, wonderful and exciting things with their minds? Do you profess to possess a greater understanding of the universe than their professors, i.e. the ones who prefix their names with 'Dr' and suffixes with a string of other acronymic letters detailing their academic, scientific and medical pursuits? 'Former-evolutionist', 'former-child actor' and 'former-atheist' don't make for good name suffixes ... not that I'm questioning your qualifications in biology and cosmology.

Was Jesus Real?

Can you seriously blame these kids, the future of your country and mine, for not taking the conjecture of someone who referred to a banana as, "the atheist's nightmare", seriously? At university, you can just walk into lectures and debates where students and teachers debate just about any subject. They have access to a plethora of information that all but refutes Jesus.

Seriously, think about it. Quirinius performed a census of the area in around before the end of the first decade of A.D. and yet there is no Jesus. Nada! Nothing! There is even a mention that Jesus, Joseph and Mary should have been in the census:

> *In those days Caesar Augustus issued a decree that a census should be taken of the entire Roman world. (This was the first census that took place while Quirinius was governor of Syria.) And everyone went to his own town to register. So Joseph also went up from the town of Nazareth in Galilee to Judea, to Bethlehem the town of David, because he belonged to the house and line of David. He went there to register with Mary, who was pledged to be married to him and was expecting a child. While they were there, the time came for the baby to be born, and she gave birth to her firstborn, a son. She wrapped him in cloths and placed him in a manger, because there was no room for them in the inn. (Luke 2:1-7)*

Someone who caused as much turmoil as Jesus was reputed to have caused should have been recorded in history AT THE TIME THAT IT TOOK PLACE, NOT JUST HUNDREDS OF YEARS AFTER THEIR DEATH. There should logically be more testimony than just that of word of mouth translated into scripture hundreds of years later. The lack of any, and I mean any (there is literally none) historical record to verify that a man named Jesus (or the Jewish equivalent name) walked the earth completely invalidates the entire narrative.

According to the Bible, Jesus stirred up all sorts of shit, he gained followers, he healed the sick and performed miracles, if he did all or any of this, or anything extraordinary, he should have been recorded somewhere. In order to be tried by Pontius Pilate, he must have shook the very foundation of the Jewish and Roman society, and yet, there is nothing written of him until hundreds of years later. I call bullshit!

So either Jesus was insignificant and people such as the apostle Paul sincerely embellished and fabricated the story to the most grand and austere degree, or there literally was no Jesus.

Some of the Gospels actually have multiple people being resurrected at the same time of Jesus as some form of celebration... did that sort of shit happen all the time back then? If not, then it should have been written down SOMEWHERE, ANYWHERE!!!

Seriously, Kirk, the convenient little fabricated story that comes prepackaged with a false history is complete fallacy. It is 100% fabricated, and fabricated by cherry picking the stories of other ancient deities who preached the same rhetoric and performed the same miracles. If Christians still believe in the biblical story of Jesus after reading this, I question your sanity, your intelligence and your literacy... and all in that order.

I'm undecided on whether the evidence supports a historical Jesus. There is a good possibility that there was someone, with a similar apocalyptic preaching

TO KIRK CAMERON

style, who was charismatic and captured the hearts and minds of many gullible people (like an ancient Ray Comfort or Joseph Smith), however there is no corroborating evidence to support any form of divinity.

Headstrong and Cocksure

You seriously had a conversation with a "headstrong teenager"? Really, I've never met one of those! And you say that she wouldn't budge from her position because Big Bang theory is more plausible than your bearded wizard 'poofing' everything into existence? You even go as far as to assert that in order to believe in religion as you see it, you would have to work against your own intellect, and you still question why *she* couldn't see the 'light'?

From what I read, the girl was telling you that while she is afraid of death, which is pretty typical for someone her age (I know I was), she could not bring herself to believe as you do, which is in direct spite of all contrary evidence and reason. The reason I keep reiterating the same line is to get it into your head that there is no evidence to suggest that any God which any civilization has ever believed in is anymore than the product of fear, philosophy and imagination (and peyote/mushrooms/marijuana). If there is no evidence, then it is safe to assume that the Bible was just the rambling conjecture of ancient desert nomads.

You call these students 'self-assured', but how can you claim to be any different? This is just hypocritical.

You say that this girl's professors had told her that life was nothing more than a cosmic accident, but this is completely and utter horse-crap, mate. You have fabricated her words. No person alive or dead knows what conditions preceded the big bang, there are plenty of theories, but they are speculative and ultimately acknowledged as exactly that. To say that this girl was told by her professor that the universe, and by extension all life, is an accident, the professor must have some impressive understanding of what preceded the big bang, which, again, is bull shit.

As far as even the brightest minds in the world know, preceding the big bang that brought the current universe (i.e. the one we exist in) into existence was literally timeless (i.e. time did not exist). In [for the sake of ease in explanation] infinity, there is the possibility that every chance will have an opportunity to bare fruit. Consider that there could have been trillions upon trillions of universes similar to the one we find ourselves in now. These universes may have thrived, or instantly re-compacted, burned or any other infinitely improbable outcome (here's to Douglass Adams). In an alternate universe Kirk, you might be the smartest being in existence. But highly unlikely. Sorry!

My point is that if not even the most brilliant people on Earth know what preceded the big bang, why would a professor teach otherwise? If not even our most incredible astrophysicists or Big Bang Cosmologists know what preceded the big bang, how can the religion of these ancient desert nomads?

Someone such as you, Kirk, who professes to know so much about what will happen to humanity for eternity after death, appears to have no concept of what eternity actually is, means, nor do you appear to comprehend its implications. It shows a particularly loathsome flair for ignorance.

Historical Jesus

You go on to talk about 'faith in Christ' but many of Jesus' messages and teachings were morally repugnant! Let's examine Jesus' teachings on peace and love, family and closeness:

> *"[Jesus Said] Do not suppose that I have come to bring peace to the earth. I did not come to bring peace, but a sword. For I have come to turn "'a man against his father, a daughter against her mother, a daughter-in-law against her mother-in-law - a man's enemies will be the members of his own household.' (Matthew 10:34-36)*

> *"He [Jesus] replied, 'I tell you that to everyone who has, more will be given, but as for the one who has nothing, even what he has will be taken away. But those enemies of mine who did not want me to be king over them – bring them here and kill them in front of me." (Luke 19:26-27).*

Where is the prolific peace loving Jesus? Where is he hiding? Oh, there it is, I found it:

> *"[Jesus says to his disciples] A new command I give you: Love one another. As I have loved you, so you must love one another. By this all men will know that you are my disciples, if you love one another." (John 13:34)*

Let's examine just how prolific that statement just is:

> *"Do not do unto others what angers you if done to you by others." (Socrates - 436-338 B.C.)*

> *"One should seek for others the happiness one desires for himself." (Buddha Siddhartha Gautama c. 563 - c. 483 B.C.)*

> *"He sought for others the good he desired for himself. Let him pass." (Egyptian Book of the Dead - 1580-1350 B.C.)*

So basically, Jesus' most prolific and peace loving rhetoric, which was later used to create the dogmatic "Jesus loves you" bilious drivel that forms the foundation of Christianity, was frigging stolen from others. More importantly, where there is no historical record from the time, which contains the name or a variation of the name Jesus of Nazareth with parents named Mary or Joseph; there is ample historical record for the Buddha and Socrates.

And you say that this girl you supposedly spoke to was 'polite and charming, but stubborn and self-righteous'? What about you? I've watched your entire YouTube catalogue mate and see very little difference between your behavior and hers, so to infer that her behavior is anything other than exemplary is simply ridiculous on your behalf! I name thee Hypocrite!

You go onto say your "heart broke for her as she walked off to her next class, attempting to live out the remainder of her days trying to find peace and pleasure before the hand of death steals it all from her". Jesus on a stick, dude; that is intense! Had it not been an abhorrent, patronizing, self-righteous ramble, it would have sounded poetic. How can you presume to know her motivation for anything beyond your little exchange? I love you, Kirk; that was one of the most conceited, self-righteous, self-assured little tirades that I've ever read!

Revelations

I'm not surprised that said young man rejected your notion of sin and judgment. I find it hard to take anything in the acid-trip Book of Revelations, seriously. While I'm sure that the author of Revelations was having a great time sailing through the skies on all of the drugs he was consuming, if anyone takes any of that shit seriously, then that marks them as a seriously a scary individual!

You've got a slaughtered lamb that is still alive with seven horns and seven eyes, a white horse, a red horse, a black horse and a pale horse whose rider is 'Death'. There are locusts which appear as warhorses, with golden crowns, men's faces, women's hair, lions' teeth, iron breastplates, wings and scorpions' tails. There is a dragon, a beast with ten horns and seven heads. This beast is given authority by the dragon and proceeds to lead the world, being worshipped alongside the dragon. Do you believe this drivel? Actually, I shouldn't say that, I'm sure that this would make a kick-ass Raymond E. Feist novel, but Revelations is fantasy. Jesus' return has been prophesied so many times now, that the threat/promise/prophesy has lost all relevance to those with sane and rational minds... you on the other hand...

So, with that said Kirk, can you seriously blame this guy for acting as though the conversation *you* forced on him was an insult to his intelligence? It most probably was!

So in the end, you had a small debate, which apparently won, and you quoted scripture to be condescending and detract from the experience. You like the Bible, Kirk? Here's a quote for you:

> *Jesus replied, "And why do you break the command of God for the sake of your tradition? For God said, 'Honor your father and mother' But you say that if a man says to his father or mother, 'Whatever help you might otherwise have received from me is a gift devoted to God,' he is not to 'honor his father' with it. Thus you nullify the word of God for the sake of your tradition. You hypocrites! Isaiah was right when he prophesied about you: 'These people honor me with their lips, but their hearts are far from me. They worship me in vain; their teachings are but rules taught by men.' and 'Anyone who curses his father or mother must be put to death.' (Matthew 15:3-9)*

Jesus was all about the Old Testament, he frigging loved it! As such, he would have believed that children who cursed their parents should be killed. How many Christians do you know that have followed Jesus' teaching? Jesus, being an Old Testament lover, clearly would have taught that bad children should be killed, how can anyone believe that his teachings were 'inspirational', 'loving' and for all the people of the world?

Such belief is not only disillusion, but it shows that the believer has a fundamental ignorance towards his or her own beliefs. After all, how can someone of the 21st century claim, on one hand, to be a follower of Jesus' teachings and on the other hand not follow Jesus' actual teachings? Jesus said it beautifully in the above verse, *"You hypocrites! ... They worship me in vain; their teachings are but rules taught by men."*

"Many of the young people in our world are on their way to Hell", you say in your smug, self assured little way. How bloody rude! I really enjoy how evangelicals preach the love of Jesus on one hand, and His complete and utter indifference towards you if you do not deliver yourself to Him in servitude, on the other. Bull-shit!

I'm sorry Kirk, but you've portrayed yourself as little more than a scared little kitten, too afraid to go out and learn about your world so you stay close to your litter-box and scratch up the couch and piss in your superiors' shoes. You are so self-assured that you accept your doctrine, of ancient desert nomads and primitive Bronze Age philosophers, as the only true version of reality. I almost started to feel sorry for you as I wrote this letter, but then I remembered that your ignorance is horrendously infectious. Science is not an easy subject to learn, mate, but when you reject it verbally then use its fruits to distribute your message, you just end up looking like a hypocrite.

Lots of Love,

Jake Farr-Wharton

TO PAT ROBERTSON

God Answers Prayer

M.G. "Pat" Robertson has achieved national and international recognition as a religious broadcaster, religious leader, businessman and author. He is the founder and chairman of The Christian Broadcasting Network (CBN) Inc. and founder of International Family Entertainment Inc., Regent University, Operation Blessing International Relief and Development Corporation, American Center for Law and Justice, The Flying Hospital, Inc., and several other organizations and broadcast entities.

Founded in 1960, CBN was the first Christian television network established in the United States. Today, CBN is one of the world's largest television ministries and produces programming seen in 200 nations and heard in 70 languages including Russian, Arabic, Spanish, French, and Chinese. CBN's flagship program, *The 700 Club*, which Robertson hosts, can be seen in 97 percent of television markets across the United States and is one of the longest running religious television shows that reaches an average of one million American viewers daily.

God Almighty answers prayer. I know what it's like.

When I was assigned to a combat division in Korea and went up to the front, my mother, who was a praying, godly woman, was on her knees crying out to God that I would be spared. And lo and behold, I was. It was a miracle I won't go into right now, but it was an absolute miracle in an assignment tent at the headquarters of the 1st Marine Division. And my mother's prayers were answered.

God Almighty answers prayers. Now here's what is said in the 91st Psalm, and we're going to be speaking on that for a few days, because our men are going – and women – are going into combat. In the 91st Psalm we read:

The protection comes from living in the shelter. It isn't a question of just getting in there real fast. You live in the shelter of the Most High. It is God Almighty who is able to keep us safe.

We want to be praying for our men and women in service. We're going to call this Operation Prayer Shield, and I want you to know, and all of us to know here in America, that if we pray – I'll be talking more about this – that we can dwell in the shadow of the Most High. And if He's giving us protection, then we have the covering.

You know in Russia, in the current situation with the Mafia being rather strong, they say to a businessman, "You need a roof. You need a roof." And the roof is either protection from one of the mobs, or it is some governmental agency that looks after you, and under that roof you are safe. And if you don't have the roof, then you're dependent on your own wits to keep you alive.

But God says, "I will provide a covering over you." He will give a covering over our nation. He will give a covering over our troops. And that's what it is we want to be talking about as we're praying for what we call Operation Prayer Shield.

These next 40 days, the days of Lent, we're asking you to begin a Lenten season and to show you're sincere to the Lord not only to pray, but also to give up something. Maybe it's sweets. Maybe it's desserts. Maybe it's watching television. Maybe it's going to the movies. Maybe you want to do a true fast. Maybe a fruit juice fast. Maybe you want to fast one meal a day. But whatever it is, do something to say to God, "I am sincere. I mean business."

We're focusing in on 40 days. We want to see a prayer shield go up around these men and women. And not only these men and women, but the United States, because the chances of somebody with a nuclear device using them against one of our cities or one of our installations is very high.

We don't know when these terrorists might strike, but it's so easy. The thousands and thousands of vulnerable targets – to pick one and blow it up and hurt people. Israel lives under this threat every day.

But we've been talking about the 91st Psalm, and it says, "Those who live in the shelter of the Most High shall abide in the shadow of the Almighty." And you need to live in His shelter. It isn't enough to say, "Well, I'm going to run in there at the last minute when there's a problem." What He says is, "You've got to live in it. You have to live in the shelter."

And then He says, "I will declare of the Lord, He is my refuge, my place of safety, my God and I'm trusting in Him." So He is a refuge and He is a place of safety, and it's interesting that we regard God, who's a person, as being a place of safety. And you live in His shelter. Now He becomes your refuge and place of safety. You're living in Him.

And then it goes on to say in the third verse, "He will rescue you from every trap and protect you from the fatal plague." So He's going to rescue you from traps and He is going to deliver you from plagues. So whatever's coming – I think this gas is a plague. But there it is. He's going to do that for you.

If you live in His shelter, you will find refuge in Him as a place of safety, and then He will rescue you from traps. Saddam Hussein has traps out there.

And He's going to also take care of you – deliver you from plagues. That's what the Bible says is going to happen to those who live in the Lord.

So take this 91st Psalm; read it; memorize it; let it be part of you. I've heard of one company where they went into battle every single day reciting the 91st Psalm, and they had no casualties. God did what He said. They trusted Him. They dwelt in the shadow of the Most High. They lived – they abided in His presence and He delivered them.

We'll talk more about His deliverance and the things that He will do, but this can be our shield for this nation and for this world. We call this Operation Prayer Shield.

Dear Pat,

Firstly, I'd like to thank you for your military service in Korea. Your country owes you a debt of gratitude. Sorry mate, but here is where the platitude ends.

Operation Bullshit Shield

Let me preface by saying, I believe you owe America an apology, namely to the families of dead American Christian soldiers who heard and believed your promise that God would "shield them through prayer". The US body count as of January 1st, 2010, since the War on Terror began in 2002, stands at 5232 dead and more than 100,000 wounded. This number, of course, does not include the hundreds of thousands of young men and women who are irreparably mentally scarred and will now depend on a lifetime of pharmaceutical and therapeutic counseling. This number is estimated to be greater than 300,000 by the Pentagon. Didn't God hear their respective prayers?

Moreover, the most recent census reveals that more than 75% of Americans self-identify as Christian. Based on the claims in your letter, the total number of dead should equal less than 1,500; physically wounded less than 25,000, and mentally injured less than 75,000. So we must ask ourselves why did your proclaimed 'Operation Prayer Shield' fail so miserably?

Why? Well, you might as well pray to brick walls (or wail into the foundations of an ancient temple) for all the good it does. There have actually been several objective and qualitative studies performed on prayer, and it may actually surprise you to hear that their findings were unanimous; prayer works... exactly zero percent of the time.

However, before we properly examine the effectiveness of prayer, I'd like to address the fact that you apparently firmly, and unflinchingly believe God to be on *our* side. 'If God can be for us, who can be against us', right? Well, do you realize the enemy is praying to the same damn God? The God of Abraham, the lover of Mary, the father of Jesus. They are sending up their prayer mail to the Lord Almighty, too. And the Koran, a book that post-dates the Bible by a good 600 years, has God promising to look after their boys fighting over there:

> *"Put thy trust in God. For God loves those who put their trust (in Him). If God helps you, none can overcome you: if He forsakes you, who is there, after that, that can help you? In God, then, let Believers put their trust." (Koran 3:159-160)*

Gotta feel a little sorry for God, eh? It's like rooting for two football teams all season and then having both qualify for the Super Bowl. Which team does He, then, put His celestial might behind? What a conundrum! Does God then hope for a 0-0 draw so as to show His impartiality? What a pickle for God when the Americans fought against Mussolini's Italians during the Second World War, the founding fathers of Christendom.

Then we have our present conflicts, in Afghanistan and Iraq, two opposing Armies meet on the battlefield praying to the same Overlord. Worse still for the Christian soldiers is the fact that the Muslims *must* pray five times a day, every day! Surely, dedication and round-the-clock obedience has to count for something, right?

Are you are one of those dudes that proclaims that, "there are no atheists in foxholes?" By the way, See, I never understood this stupid little meme, as it suggests that all soldiers are God followers, which implies that every soldier killed in his foxhole, did so praying to his God for help. Further evidence that suggests that prayer is an obvious exercise in futility. So what about the believing soldiers who prayed to God before going into their fox hole? You insinuated that they should have had some form of shield sustained by God around them, protecting them from gun fire... and yet statistically, cases where Christians were protected by a shield are on par with the number of times Wile Coyote got the Road Runner- exactly zero!

Let's imagine for a moment, the face of a fictional 19 year old Daniel, from Nebraska who never stepped foot outside of his home state prior to commencing boot camp in the months before being deployed to Baghdad. He has been in-country for only a week and is on his first foot patrol of Sadr City, a city teaming with enemy combatants and blood thirsty Al-Qaeda insurgents. It is just on nightfall when all of a sudden "BAM!! Ratta-tat-tat. BAM" Daniel's platoon is ambushed in a narrow street surrounded by high walls in all directions. It's not yet quite clear where the enemy fire is coming from, but for these young, inexperienced men, it is if a million AK-47s, mortars, and RPG's are pointed directly down on their position; and the may well be.

The air is thick with flying metal. Confusion and panic sets in and soon delirium grips him. Smoke makes it difficult to tell friend from foe. The startled platoon runs in all directions, desperately seeking temporary sanctuary from the mayhem.

Daniel, a devout Christian, dives into an abandoned shop front for cover. For a few seconds, he is relieved. Comforted that he made it off the street alive and out of the line of enemy fire. Then suddenly the heart sinking realization that he has been separated from the rest of his men hits him. The adrenalin pumping through his veins that has sustained him this far is making him jumpy and twitchy.

His heart is almost pounding out of his chest. He can now hear voices but not the soothing reassuring sounds of a Texas drawl or a Tennessee twang, but the whispers of indecipherable Arabic. The hushed tones get closer and closer. He realizes that his position must now be known to the enemy, and in moments, he will be in a life or death firefight against an unknown number of combatants with unknown firepower. This moment of sheer terror this 19 year old from Nebraska is one that most of us will never experience. The fear makes his eyes as wide as dinner plates, but he is able to shut them for a second in a desperate effort to call upon God to spare him.

Pat, let's now pretend that God hears this frightened boy's pleas. For God to intervene he would now have to set in motion a chain of events that runs in direct contravention of the known plan that God, being the omniscient sentient being that he is, had already put in place when he created the Universe. Considering that God wrote the rule book, and all the pieces at play within it - God would have already taken into account all his needs and desires when he made his original decision on this soldier's fate.

Think about it. You have to admit there is something intrinsically strange about the idea of God changing his mind or changing the course of events in mid-battle. You imply that God is omniscient, and to be omniscient means that for every decision that he has made, there cannot arise any new or additional information that God failed to take into consideration that might make him change his mind or reverse course, for he knows *everything about everything*.

As tragic and dire this soldier's fate would appear to be, it is utterly intellectually preposterous to believe that God not only listens to his prayer but also then completely circumvents the natural laws to cater for his whim. Surely you acknowledge this?

The Science of Prayer

Let us examine the futility of prayer from a scientific perspective. By doing this, unfortunately for your faith, we can prove that prayer fails 100% of the time. How? By eliminating ambiguity and coincidence from a miraculously claimed scenario and by miraculous I mean – anytime that the laws of nature are suspended or circumvented, which (apart from the fairytales of the Old Testament) is literally never, ever.

This is best demonstrated on a brilliant website *www.whywontgodhealamputees.com*.

Let's imagine that your doctor has diagnosed you with an aggressive form of malignant bowel cancer. You opt to take the chemotherapy that your doctor is recommending and as this god awful remedy of radiation exposure begins you are naturally terrified at the prospect that the number of your days on Earth are dramatically falling. Assuming you are a Christian, you begin to pray to God or Jesus for some divine intervention and thus you pray morning and night, before, during and after surgery that your heavenly father will spare you an early visit to the grave.

A few months after the chemo your doctor is delighted to tell you that you have survived the cancer and all signs of the life threatening disease have now vanished. Naturally, you give thanks to God for heeding your prayers and your conviction and faith in Jesus is stronger than ever before. Praise the Lord, it's a frigging miracle!

But how do we objectively rationalize the above scenario? What saved you from seemingly imminent doom? Well there are several possibilities. Was it the surgery, radiation therapy, your body's natural defense (or all of those), or was it God's interference? On the surface, the answer to this question seems ambiguous. God may have miraculously cured your disease, as many Christians would believe. But if God is fictional then it had to be either the chemotherapy, surgery and/or your natural immune system that cured you – which, given the number of atheists, agnostics, Hindus,

Buddhists, Pagans or theistic ambivalent who are healed from equally aggressive cancer every day, is more likely. Call me a skeptic, if you like.

For argument's sake though, there is only one way to remove the coincidence of prayer working when medicine doesn't and that is to eliminate this inherent ambiguity. In an un-ambiguous situation, there is no potential for coincidence. Because there is no ambiguity, we can actually *know* whether God is answering the prayer or not. The examination of faithful amputees allows us to completely remove all of this inherent vagueness, and in doing so create a clear-cut situation that we can see with our own eyes and prove unequivocally that prayer simply does not work. Therefore, we can be sure that whenever a believer has proclaimed instances of miraculous healing through prayer we can be certain that the possibility of coincidence was present.

What we find is that whenever we remove ambiguity from a situation like this, and meticulously examine the results of prayer, the evidence shows, unequivocally, that prayer has no outcome, neither positive nor negative. Put in another way, when you remove the possibility of coincidence, God simply does not answer. Put another way still, either God holds some serious disdain for amputees, or there is probably no God.

With that said, any parent, including myself, can understand the frantic desire for divine intervention when their child is sick. But prayer is not and will never be an equivalent to or a substitute for medical intervention. Seriously, wishing your God to save your sick child is like trying to attack a heavily fortified castle by putting your children in a giant slingshot and flinging them at it – you end up looking like a fool and your children get injured, if not killed in the process.

Far too many children have been killed by their faith-blinded parents who were relying on prayer and faith healing. It is people like you that need to be held accountable for perpetuating the absolute fallacy that prayer and miracles work. Allow me to further illustrate, using the parents of 11-year-old Madeline Kara Neumann as case in point. Her Mom and Dad prayed for a 'miracle' to cure her of the most treatable form of childhood onset diabetes. Madeline's conditioned worsened, becoming sicker and sicker, until she died. The autopsy determined that she had died from diabetic ketoacidosis, an ailment that left her with too little insulin in her body. As with all cases of Type I diabetes diagnosed since the development of injected insulin, this would have been treated by regular insulin injections. In other words, a miracle wasn't needed, just an ounce of rationality.

Madeline would have joined the other 1 in 700 children diagnosed with Type I Diabetes that, by in large, go on to live normal and mostly healthy lives, but instead, her moronic parents decided that instead of seeking medical attention they would pray to the king of the pixies. Madeline was intensely sick for no less than around a month before she finally succumbed to her very treatable illness. Her last 30 days would have been filled with nausea, vomiting, excessive thirst, and loss of appetite and extreme weakness. The parents commented that God did not help their daughter because *"we did not have enough faith."*

What can you say about such a case? You could try saying, "I'm sure this is an isolated case", but you would be both wrong and obscenely uninformed.

Seriously, are you so self indulgent and arrogant to believe that God favored you over the tens of thousands of fellow US Marines that were laid to waste on the Korean Peninsula? What makes you so special? I'd like to hear from you on this. 'God saved' plenty of budding Scientologists and Buddhists in Korea also, do you think it's cause they prayed harder to emperor Xenu than the tens of thousands of good Christian men and boys who died?

Prayer Doesn't Work in Africa... or for the Jewish

Are you aware that today while you are busy telling your CBC viewers that homosexuality and abortion are responsible for the decline of society in America (which, I imagine, is what you do most days), another 30,000 infants and toddlers on the African continent will die of dehydration? Their anonymous tongues splitting in half in the days before their inevitable and excruciating anonymous deaths on some anonymous sand pit with the sun and wind blasting a 110 degree furnace onto their tiny little bodies! Perhaps they just hadn't found God... or not the right God. Perhaps they didn't know to pray. Perhaps they weren't praying hard enough.

Or consider that we can assume that an overwhelming majority of the six million Jews for certain sent panic stricken desperate prayers of plea in the moments prior to being marched into a ditch, tossed into an oven, or ushered into a gas chamber. ALL of those hundreds of millions of prayers went unheeded, completely ignored by THEIR OWN God, your God! The God of the

Israelites, of the Hebrews, the God of Abraham, that delivered them from Egypt, that decimated innumerable armies that amassed against them (as reputed in the Old Testament). Do you think God had a little bit of magic up his wizard's sleeve for special ole you when he spared your life in Korea? Are you beginning to see how outrageously egotistical it is to purport such sentiments?

Are you are one of those people that can read a news story about a plane crash and mutter aloud, "what a miracle that that little girl survived. God blessed her."? But what of the other 250 passengers that were either burnt alive in their seats from the squirting jet fuel, or crushed to death? Some miracle huh? Wouldn't a loving God see this accident occurring ahead of time and opt spare all? Wouldn't that be far greater proof for God's existence of benevolence?

I am aware that Jesus says in the Bible that prayer works and that it should be done regularly, but let's be honest, he wasn't the sharpest tool in the shed. The New Testament is filled with a plethora of his false promises; notwithstanding the big porky he told when he promised his followers he'd return before they'd die... oops! The Apostle Paul made the same promise (that Jesus would return to take all followers to his castle in the clouds) to the far-flung churches he'd established, after they'd grown weary of the bullshit. Unfortunately, Jesus never came back for them, or any of the other rapture ready Christians since then. Actually, I wrote a song about that, you can download it on iTunes called, *If You're Rapture Ready, Say Amen*.

Throughout the gospels of the New Testament, Jesus promises many times that he will answer the prayers of the masses. For example, in *Matthew 7:7* Jesus says:

"Ask, and it will be given you; seek, and you will find; knock, and it will be opened to you. For every one who asks receives, and he who seeks finds, and to him who knocks it will be opened. Or what man of you, if his son asks him for bread, will give him a stone? Or if he asks for a fish, will give him a serpent? If you then, who are evil, know how to give good gifts to your children, how much more will your Father who is in heaven give good things to those who ask him!"

In fact, Jesus makes seventeen references to the unyielding efficacy of prayer throughout Matthew, Mark, Luke, and John. Ask and you will receive. But why don't faithful, God fearing, Jesus loving amputees get their limbs restored? Oh yeah, we covered that, didn't we?

Situations where prayer brings about a solution or a positive result are well understood and well researched:

"If you want something to happen you pray to make it happen and what you're really doing is setting yourself up to be super aware of that proposed solution. If you pray for a particular object and all of a sudden you find it, it doesn't mean the prayer works, only that you were aware to the possibility of that object." (Ed Keinholz)

That said, often, people who pray, pray for silly little things that would have easily come to fruition without the need for prayer. Things like recovering from heart surgery, recovery from a car accident, recovery from cancer, recovery from swine flu or whatever other ailments you can think of. People swear by homeopathy for exactly the same reason; it is literally as potent as tap water; it contains no active ingredients and has absolutely no possibility of affecting anyone's health, positively or negatively, on any level, yet people swear by it.

If someone suggests that their liver was cured of cirrhosis after months of prayer you should punch them in the damn throat! It could never have been the strictly followed diet that their doctor gave them, cessation of all drugs and alcohol and the introduction of exercise for the first time in their life, and it most definitely wasn't because the liver is the fastest healing organ in the body... no it must have been the prayer!

If you want people (outside of religion) to take prayer seriously, get a billion of your fellow God-guzzling brothers and sisters to make *just one* limb of *one* person grow back. Not 'heal' cancer, not wake from a coma, but properly, incontrovertibly, irrefutably total re-growth of a human limb. Just one, and I promise you, I'll believe you!

Such claims disgust me more than the weird lumps of moldy food under my daughter's bed! All you need to do is turn the TV over to a current affairs program or Faux News channel (I am not advocating the use of Fox News, Fox News should only be watched in small doses and if propaganda induced paranoia persists, please see Keith Olberman) to see the latest 'empirical evidence' for prayer healing the sick or raising the dead. We're taught by parents and pastors, that prayer will some how enrich our life and bring us closer to God, but there is literally no effect to be experienced, by anyone, ever!

As much as you and your brethren like to promote the efficacy of prayer, Pat, the evidence works inordinately against you. Take me, for instance, from the ages of 12-18 I was a living, breathing, praying-machine! I even went to a youth prayer camp, where literally all you do is eat, sleep, pray and eat (I was especially good at the eating part). Despite all of my concentrated efforts, Pamela Anderson never arrived on my doorstep offering to take my virginity; my parents never bought me a vintage cherry red Mustang convertible; my Christian rock band "The Shades" never made it past the first round in local 'Battle of the Bands' competitions (possibly because we literally dressed like the wiggles); and I never arbitrarily tripped over a wallet, returned it to its rightful owner and then subsequently given a billion dollars in reward money! What further proof do you need, Pat?

Pat, people like you utterly disgust me. All you do is pray on the insecurities of others; wake up! Stop peddling false hope of an invisible, intangible and uncaring product. If you truly have altruistic goals then help people with *real* practical help that does not unnecessarily place them in harm's way as in the case of little Madeline Kara Neumann. Do some charity work without proselytizing, house some homeless people and help orphans find homes.

While you're praying, I'm doing something useful.

Faithfully yours,

Jake Farr-Wharton

TO DR. GEORGIA PURDOM

Irreducible Stupidity

Dear Reader, the following is an article by Dr. Georgia Purdom, Ph.D. (molecular genetics Ohio State University). Despite her field of expertise, she is a proponent of Intelligent Design Creationism. She is an active contributor for Creation Ministries International and Answers in Genesis and actively writes against the enemies of Christianity and Intelligent Design Creationism - namely that of intelligence, rationality and credible scientific research and discovery. Her full address can be found here:

www.answersingenesis.org/articles/am/v1/n1/intelligent-design-movement

The Intelligent Design (ID) movement has gained increasing recognition and publicity over the last several years at both local and national levels. It is especially well-known in educational realms, where it has been heralded as an alternative to Darwinism/naturalism.

The historical roots of the ID movement lie in the natural theology movement of the eighteenth and nineteenth centuries. The current movement, however, uses more than just philosophical arguments for a designer; it uses scientific evidences drawn from biology, chemistry and physics.

ID uses irreducible complexity (meaning that for something to function, it still requires a certain number of parts), to infer that living and nonliving things have been designed. These biological pathways consist of many factors, and all the factors are necessary for the pathway to function properly. Thus, evolution—which works via the mechanism of small, gradual steps and keeping only that which is immediately functional—could not have formed these pathways. Evolution is goalless and purposeless; therefore, it does not keep the leftovers.

The question of whether or not a feature of a living organism displays irreducible complexity is answered by using what is called an "explanatory filter." The filter has three modes of explanation:

1. Necessity: Did it have to happen?
2. Chance: Did it happen by accident?
3. Design: Did an intelligent agent cause it to happen?

This is a very logical, common-sense approach used by individuals every day to deduce cause and effect. A feature of the universe or a living organism must be designed if the first two modes of explanation are answered as no.

William Dembski states, "ID is three things: a scientific research program that investigates the effects of intelligent causes; an intellectual movement that challenges Darwinism and its naturalistic legacy; and a way of understanding divine action." The ID theory focuses on what is designed rather than answering the questions of who, when, why, and how. Those within the movement believe this promotes scientific endeavor by looking for function and purpose in those things that are designed; whereas an evolutionary mindset presupposes waste and purposelessness and aborts further scientific investigation.

ID may serve as a useful tool in preliminary discussions about God and creation to gain an audience that might be turned off at the mention of the Bible. Since the movement is very careful not to associate itself with Christianity or any formal religion, some think it will stand a better chance of gaining acceptance as an alternative to Darwinism in the schools. The movement has produced many resources that support the biblical creationist viewpoint. It makes clear that Darwinism/naturalism is based on the presupposition that the supernatural does not exist, thus affecting the way one interprets the scientific evidence.

Without the framework of the Bible and the understanding that evil entered the world through man's actions (*Genesis 3*), God appears sloppy and incompetent. People ask why God is unable to prevent evil from thwarting His plans, resulting in such poor design, instead of understanding that because of the Fall there is now a cursed design.

God's role as Creator is foundational to His role as Redeemer.

When trusting the Bible as opposed to neglecting it, we read that Jesus clearly conquered death with the Resurrection (*Romans 6:3–10*) and that one day death will no longer reign (*Revelation 21:4*). Again, the Creator and the creation reflect on each other.

The Creator and His creation cannot be separated; therefore, knowledge of God must come through both general revelation (nature) and special revelation (the Bible). The theologian Louis Berkhof said, "... since the entrance of sin into the world, man can gather true knowledge about God from His general revelation only if he studies it in the light of Scripture." It is only then that the entire truth about God and what is seen around us can be fully understood and used to help people understand the bad news in Genesis and the good news of Jesus Christ.

Dear Georgia,

While I concede that your doctorate awards you the title 'doctor' I am reluctant to refer to you as one due to your anti-evolution insistence. I am especially perplexed by your belief in intelligent design and creationism given your specific field of specialty.

From Oxford Online Encyclopedia:

> *Molecular genetics is the field of biology that studies the structure and function of genes at a molecular level. The field studies how the genes are transferred from generation to generation. Molecular genetics employs the methods of genetics and molecular biology. Along*

with determining the pattern of descendants, molecular genetics helps in understanding genetic mutations that can cause certain types of diseases. Through utilizing the methods of genetics and molecular biology, molecular genetics discovers the reasons why traits are carried on and how and why some may mutate.

Cognitive Dissonance

Given your field of expertise, I am utterly bewildered that you have rejected evolution. You are able to see mutations and understand them, able to see the manifestations of specific mutations in an organism, yet your stance on evolution makes you a complete enemy of science and reason. Instead of furthering human understanding of biological pathways, you are legitimizing the claims of morons.

In scientific research, there are the revolutionaries who change the status quo, people like Carl Woese from the University of Illinois, who has theorized a form of evolution, which essentially may have been in play before Darwinian evolution (evolution by way of natural selection); you have those who continue to validate old theorem; and you have fools who deny all evidence in favor of fairy tales.

When you look at the Human Genome, you can see our genetic history from proteomic slush, to multi-cellular eukaryotes (organisms with cell nuclei, like plans and animals). We have 23,000 protein-coding genes, which only equates to 1.5% of the genomic codes in our body. The rest is mostly (around 95%) 'Junk DNA'.

'Junk DNA' relates to DNA that has no identifiable function (at present), kind of like man boobs. While it remains to be proven, many biologists and molecular geneticists understand the 'junk' to be an evolutionary artifact, remnants of humanity's past incarnations.

To a molecular geneticist, this should make ultra-super-complete-uber-perfect sense! After all, when *they* look at the genetic code of any other plants and animals, bacteria or viruses, it becomes freaking obvious that every species on Earth has similarities. Even a redneck should be able to join the dots... if all eukaryotes have common ancestors, we should have many of the same molecular traits. We do.

Bam!

ID is Gaining Ground?

You mention, firstly, that the ID movement is gaining recognition and publicity and I would tend to agree with you. However, by no means has it ever, and will in no way gain any form of legitimacy. You can tell a billion people that everything that science says is wrong because it's not supported by your scientific text book, the Bible... but it doesn't matter how many people believe something, if there is no evidence to support it (such as in the case of ID) then it will never be true/correct/real/empirical/substantiated/validated/q uantified... except in Texas and Kansas... and Iran.

Interestingly, if we were to take the Bible in any sort of literal sense, we find that God actually performs the first case human cloning using the DNA from Adam's rib *(Genesis 2:21–22)*. So why does Christianity have so many troubles with human cloning?

The Bible is not a science textbook; it is not even a good history textbook. In fact, the first time that there is any historical accuracy is in Kings. Not a single archeological dig run in Egypt found any evidence which even slightly supported the biblical claim that the Israelites (ancient Hebrews, 12 Tribes or Jews) cohabitated with the Egyptians. The Egyptians were meticulous record keepers, and yet there is bugger all in their testimony relating to the Israelites. There is no evidence of the Israelites spending any time in the Sinai, despite their supposed 40-year tenure. While absence of evidence doesn't specifically guarantee evidence of absence, you'd expect to see *something*, right? Nonetheless, this lone fact totally invalidates the Exodus in my humble view.

The claims made in Genesis can be just as easily refuted. There is unique biodiversity on every continent, which ultimately suggests there was no global flood, nor is there any geological evidence to support such a flood. There are also funny little tidbits like the proclamation that God created the plants on one day, then the sun the day after... um hello? The plants would have frozen solid. Oh, and in Genesis 2, God creates light, and then creates the stars in the Heavens. Nice work there, God!

To put it succinctly, the Old Testament has exactly the same amount of evidence to support its historicity and claims as Harry Potter, Cinderella or Tinkerbelle, but is far less entertaining!

Scholars Suggest

I love that you say that ID is especially "well-known in educational realms, where it has been heralded as an alternative to Darwinism/naturalism". I'm sorry to have to say this so early on, but seriously, retract your head from the velvety folds of your anus and smell the bullshit! Exactly who, beyond the peons of Christ have regarded ID as any form of alternative to evolution by way of natural selection?

ID is not an alternative to Darwinism, it's the antithesis of Darwinism. In fact, it is the freaking antithesis of science. It is, however, the alternative to doing your homework in high school:

Mom: "Bryan, have you done your physics and chemistry homework? I want to check it before you hand it in tomorrow."

Bryan: "Yeah, Mom, I just answered 'God did it' for every question and when it asked for the calculated difference between Gallium and Germanium, I wrote, 'the Bible says you're an asshole'."

Mom: "Somebody's getting chocolate sprinkles on their ice cream tonight!"

How dare you claim that ID is any form of alternative to anything but freaking rationality! It gains support from kids who were home schooled by parents too afraid to send their children to schools where they'd mix with other children with 'dangerous ideas'. By "dangerous ideas", I mean 'normal' children who have been taught correctly, that the earth is older than 6,000 years, or worse… they could be Muslims!

I say that in jest of course, I'm sure that there are plenty of reputable people out there who believe that ID is an alternative to evolution, right? A 2009 poll, by Pew Research Centre, found that 87% of scientists say that humans and other living things have evolved over time and that evolution is the result of natural processes such as natural selection. Of course, some of these scientists could be simple technicians with a science degree; I think we can do better.

Actually, a Newsweek poll of 480,000 scientists [in the fields of biology and geology] found that 99.85% of America's earth and life scientists 'believe' in evolution. That means that only .15% of people with a proper understanding of evolution actually reject evolutionary science that's pretty small Georgia...

So, to whom, exactly, were you referring to when you claimed that, "is especially 'well-known in educational realms, where it has been heralded as an alternative to Darwinism/naturalism.'?" I live in Australia, Georgia, and I can smell the buuuuullshit from all the way over here... and it smells nutty!

Historically Bullshit

As you say, the roots of the ID movement come from the eighteenth and nineteenth century, but does this give it legitimacy? No. The old 'every watch has a watchmaker; therefore everything must have a creator', (ergo God) is the one of the most hilarious logical fallacies that has permeated the hearts and minds of ridiculously idiotic people all over the world. The hilarious problem with this argument is that it has no end, and the proponents of ID don't seem to have realized it. If all creations must have a creator then God must have also had a creator, and God's god must have also had a creator and so on up the chain to some sort of council of mega-gods.

Hey, I think I just invented a new religion, and because I'd be worshiping the gods that created the Christian, Jewish and Muslim God. My god would be infinitely more powerful. All I'd have to do is write a doctrine and I could do that based on the Abrahamic religion's texts from the perspective that anything that God did, my god told him... or her to do it. I digress.

Bad Science

You say that the current arguments use scientific evidence drawn from biology, chemistry and physics. Hmm, well, if it uses science, it must be true, right?

Irreducible Complexity is the bastard child of Creationist Michael Behe. Behe, apart from having a surname that when spoken sounds like a fat guy laughing, hypothesized that certain organisms have biological systems that are too complex to have evolved from simpler, or "less complete" predecessors through mutations i.e. natural selection.

Irreducible Complexity uses 'sciencey' terminology (which is a term I've coined to describe something which sounds like science, but looks like dog shit) and a convoluted form of Scientific Method (the linear process by which scientifically reputable theorem are developed, scrutinized and published), and explains that many organisms - such as Intelligent Design's slutty poster child, the Bacterial Flagellum - could not have survived any form of evolution process do to their inability to do *anything* without their complete biological system intact as we see it today. Put in another way, these Irreducibly Complex organisms are supposedly un-evolvable – or they could not have ever come about through a process of evolution. The Bacterial Flagellum is an easy organism to suggest this of, mainly because it looks so darn mechanical, and because every machine must have had an engineer, and every design a designer. Speaking of which, what do you think I should call my new mega-god? Think I'll name it after my favorite cartoon from the 80s; I name her 'Thundercat'! I digress too much.

If you have a complex, single or multi-cellular biochemical machine, which is composed of many parts, its function can *ABSOLUTELY* be favored by natural selection. But the argument is that evolution cannot produce them because the individual parts have no function of their own, thus they are Irreducibly Complex. Therefore, you can't evolve a structure like the bacterial flagellum.

So how does evolution explain this? Well, even Darwin - who didn't have access to dinosaur fossils, genomics or electron microscopes; whose theory of natural selection took almost an entire lifetime of observation and experimentation - had a method of understanding this. The complicated machines, simply do not arise as they are, they arise from different components or structures that have different functions of their own. Each component or structure originates with functions of its own and natural selection favors those components that help the components to survive. If the organism can better survive because it has a shoulder mounted mini-gun, then the organism has a greater chance of passing on its DNA to the next generation, where the shoulder mounted mini-gun gene may be dominant and thus manifest, and then passed down again and again. If irreducible complexity is right, then the parts of these complex organisms, like in the case of the Bacterial Flagellum (as you, Georgia and Michael Behe have surmised), should be absolutely useless, should die, and should have no chance of reproduction to pass on its sexy Flagellum DNA. If evolution is correct, however, then we should be able to look at these bits and pieces that make up the organism to discover further functionality.

Here's the kicker (and many thanks to P.Z. Meyers for pointing this out), if you take the motor like mechanism and tail *off* the bacterial flagellum - removing forty of the fifty proteins which comprise it - it is still a functional organism. At its reduced capacity, what remains is a "Type III Secretary System" or in lay terms, a molecular syringe. It is not a flagellum (as its ability to move has now been removed) but it is still a bacteria. At this stage of 'irreducible complexity', the bacterium is still able to inject toxin into human cells quite efficiently. In fact, the bacterium that causes the bubonic plague is no different to this altered bacterial flagellum.

Gary: "Did he just disprove Irreducible Complexity, making those ID proponents look like complete fool-tards?"

Greg: "I think he did, Gary, I think he did!"

Me: "Eeps, sorry, I didn't mean to make you look like fool-tards using the science you perverted in order to create your convoluted theory."

ID Gets Out-Evidenced

We now reach a beautiful point of conclusion where I get to say, in my best Richard Dawkins impression; "the arguments of Intelligent Design, the ones that use scientific method to refute evolution, do not stand up to scientific scrutiny". Irreducible Complexity sounds science-y, it looks science-y, but it is, in fact... religion-y! Irreducible Complexity is maliciously false, fallacious, fallacy and factually bereft. 'Irreducible Complexity' is to 'viable scientific theory' as 'fun' is to 'lighting yourself on fire'; metaphorically speaking, of course.

When I was an uber-Christian (you heard me, I used to be a Fundy McChristian) but had started to lose touch with the Good Book over its inability to stand up to scientific scrutiny, I fell deeply in love with irreducible complexity. It was the best of both worlds, you see. It appears to use very complex science, whilst rationally demonstrating there is an absolutely need for a creator. The best part is, of course, you get to sound smart at the same time as being able to sleep with pious Christian girls who would otherwise kick you in the crotch for not respecting their commitment to Christ. Intelligent Design, making stupid people look smart since 1996.

Problem is though, just because it looks like science and speaks like science; it doesn't necessarily mean that it is science.

Blind Goalies

Georgia, you say that evolution is goalless and purposeless, WTF? I mean sure, it's not as though the many reputable scientists and researchers who have painstakingly tested and retested evolution, since it was originally theorized a little over 150 years ago, were trying to understand our origins or anything, right? Hang on! Goalless? I can't imagine a better goal or purpose than understanding our own freaking origins!

If you think the key to understanding our past is in a book written by desert nomads 4-5000 years before the earth was discovered to be spherical, you're delusional. And, considering the amount of time and effort you've put into your education you certainly appear to be equal parts delusional and dense. Goalless... pft!

Infinite Probability

Your little explanatory filter questions are hilariously stupid and honestly suggest a complete lack of understanding in evolutionary biology and it's interdependence on both virtually limitless time and the natural laws. It just doesn't make sense.

Necessity: Did it have to happen? No. It happened because the conditions were right. I suppose though, that my answer is simplistic. After all, we know from our observations that given enough time, every statistical improbability has a chance to exert or present its self. As such, while no event *has* to happen, given enough time, it probably will anyway. Did I just blow your mind?

Chance: Did it happen by accident? No, it happened because of an external stimuli occurring under the right conditions; heat, radiation, cold, pressure. Was it photosynthesis or chemosynthesis or something else that we've not yet discovered? In the 1980s and 1990s, biologists found that certain types of microbial life had an incredible ability that allowed it to not only survive, but thrive in extreme environments. Suddenly, niches such as the extraordinarily hot, or acidic – areas which were previously thought to be completely inhospitable to complex organisms – were found to harbour exactly that, complex organisms. Some scientists even concluded that life may have begun on Earth in hydrothermal vents far under the ocean's surface.

I've discussed primordial earth and the possible formations of the first RNA and DNA in another letter; I suggest you take a read.

Design: Did an intelligent agent cause it to happen? No, there is no evidence to suggest that there is a creator beyond that which you create to explain that which you do not understand yet. Georgia, the only reason that you would submit to the notion of a creator is if you were predisposed to such belief (i.e. indoctrinated at an early age) or you were unable to understand the contrary evidence. Considering your qualifications, I doubt that you are unable to understand evolution. Your biography says that you became a Christian at a youth camp when you were 8, an age where you are old enough to reason, but not specifically old enough to wade through the bullshit and discern fact.

While your filter questions may well be logical and have a common-sense approach, they are simplistic. While they may work for filtering everyday situations to deduce cause and effect, they certainly do not prove a creator of the universe. To suggest such would be ridiculous. All you've done is create a series of painfully convoluted non-sequiturs.

You say that 'a feature of the universe or a living organism must be designed if the first two modes of explanation are answered as no', but again, the questions are far too simplistic to apply to living organisms or geological phenomena. Again, regardless of improbability, given enough time, every possible event has a chance to occur.

Please indulge me a small digression from this topic for a minute to touch on an important overarching theme.

Here's 'the thing', Georgia, We humans have this innate ability to connect the dots, even when there are none. This leads the vast majority of humans to feel an overwhelming need to purge themselves of the scourge of Ignorance. For them, and also apparently you, Georgia, 'not knowing' something is such an overwhelming abhorrence and as such, must be answered. But, you're not alone in this.

Experiments with birds in their nesting phase have proven interesting. If you provide it with a choice between its own eggs and larger plastic eggs, with artificially attractive blue polka dots, it is completely unable to refuse the 'prettier egg', at the expense of its own eggs.

In experiments with butterflies, whereby a painted cardboard tube with more stripes on its underside than a natural butterfly is placed in front of a male butterfly, have shown equally interesting results. Despite the fact that the cardboard tube has no wings, the male butterfly chose to mate with the cardboard tube instead of the female butterfly.

In contrast, humans are equipped with a massive cerebral cortex which enables us to be skeptical of our environment, it enables us to realize that we're sitting on large blue plastic eggs or trying to mate with a piece of cardboard over one of our own species (except those of our species who purposely buy 'life-like' latex or plastic dolls to mate with).

With that said though, while our brains were indeed designed by evolution to be skeptical of our surroundings (i.e. hear a twig break in the savannah and assume it is a lion stalking you in the bushes), this evolutionary advantage also provided us with a significant drawback; we inherited this compulsion to fill an 'I don't know', (i.e. our ignorance) with an answer.

ID, superstition and religious belief are simply 'connecting the dots' where there are none. Carl Sagan called this "dangerous evolutionary baggage." Inserting supernatural explanations in the place of natural ones would have made perfect sense when early hominids were trying to survive in a world where everything was trying to eat them.

Due to the fact that our 'instincts' are still demonstrably strong, religion is still a most prevalent superstition; as a species, we still continue to ascribe supernatural explanations to our very natural lives. We still connect the dots, even when, like with ID, there most assuredly are none.

The point of this digression is to simply point out that ignorance is not only ok, but it is literally the driving force behind science. Georgia, that is something that you seem to have forgotten. You cannot go into scientific research with the presupposition that there is a creator behind it all; it is dishonest and creates a bias, which invalidates the findings.

When humanity stood up, with the avid curiosity that *really* defines us as a species, and tried to understand the world around us, we found many answers. We have so much more to go, we have so much that we do not know; it is ignorance, which drives us forward. Embrace it, Georgia, don't be scared of it and support the bullshit of Intelligent Design.

The Truth of ID

You quote William Dembski in order to promote your cause, he states that, "ID is three things: a scientific research program that investigates the effects of intelligent causes; an intellectual movement that challenges Darwinism and its naturalistic legacy; and a way of understanding divine action." This is factually incorrect.

ID is not a scientific research program; it uses the philosophical ramblings of ancient desert nomads to promote a scientifically bereft philosophy. Philosophy is not scientific! It is ethereal. Of course, many scientific theories come from absent and creative musings which might be considered as philosophy. The difference, though, is that once a scientific theory is established and validated, it is tested, and retested, and retested. ID works on the premise that there is a creator; a premise that is completely un-testable. And where is this illustrious creator? Oh that's right, no one's seen him since Moses.

ID is not an intellectual movement, it's a *bowel movement* made by pseudo intellectuals trying to legitimize their pseudoscience. ID may have been proposed by intellectuals who were capable of logic and reason, but instead of using their logic and reason for good, they used it for evil! ID does not challenge Darwinism, it ignores it. It places its hands over its eyes and ears and places its foot in its mouth and defecates, and calls it thesis!

Lastly, ID isn't a way of understanding divine action, it is a way of linking the ancient assertions of deities, to a form of pseudoscience in an attempt to attract those who are losing their religious faith (due to scientific discovery or rational thought), but have perhaps been given the impression that science is not worthy of their trust... and religion is.

ID is not and never will be legitimate for one very big and important reason, it is based on the assumption of a creator. An assertion there is LITERALLY NO EVIDENCE TO SUPPORT. It is not provable, reproducible theory and as such is not scientifically legitimate, so blow it out your tail pipe!

I'm Skeptical

You state that "the ID theory focuses on what is designed rather than answering the questions of who, when, why, and how," but this is because all those little facets of ID are completely unverifiable. It's not as though ID works with already validated theory to expand human understanding and knowledge, no, it ignores everything we've learned about the natural nature of nature, in favor of "God did it!"

You mention that "ID may serve as a useful tool in preliminary discussions about God and creation to gain an audience that might be turned off at the mention of the Bible," but this only confirms my assertion that all ID is, is a way to link stupidity with people that are predisposed to believing stupid things. Correlation DOES NOT prove causation. You're effectively using the evidence in the reduction of pirates to validate the Flying Spaghetti Monster (if you don't get this reference, Google Flying Spaghetti Monster). You're using sleight of hand pseudoscience in an attempt to validate your assertions of a creator. You're making baseless assumptions and non-sequiturs and using them to validate your ridiculously ignorant view of the world.

I laughed when you wrote that proponents of ID try very hard to disassociate ID with Christianity or any formal religion. Haven't you noticed, Georgia, that ID is a 'theory' that *only* Christians believe in. If you really think that this equates to ID gaining acceptance as an alternative to Darwinism in schools then you are really underestimating the intelligence of those in the education system. 'Darwinist evolution' is taught in schools, not because it sounded really smart n' shit, but because it is verified scientific theorem.

You say that the ID movement has produced many resources that support the biblical creationist viewpoint; this is, again, true. Go to any Christian bookstore in the western world and you can get some really great picture books with humans and dinosaurs cohabitating, it's frigging awesome! Didn't you know that Jesus rode into Jerusalem, not on a donkey, but on a Velociraptor? I used to watch a cartoon called Dino Wars where humans retrofitted dinosaurs with laser weapons and mind control apparatus and rode around the Earth blowing the shit out of their enemy... but it is just as fictional as the stories in the Bible.

You can produce all of the research papers on ID as you like, you can claim whatever you like, you can ever claim that quantum theory and cosmology is incorrect "because God says so". There is a good reason, however, why these so called resources will never be published in reputable scientific journals... because they're not science!

Darwinism/naturalism is not based on presuppositions that the supernatural does not exist, as you suggest. Darwinism makes no claims for or against the existence of the supernatural, which is a leap each person must make for him or her self. Some people look at a butterfly and see the wonderful work of a creator. Others look at that same butterfly and ponder the trials and tribulations that the ancestors of that species had to endure in order to find its self where it is. They wonder what purpose the color serves, when it acquired the ability to fly and where natural selection will take it in the distant future.

Creationist and evolutionist alike have access to the exact same information; their interpretations are based on their predispositions rather than their presuppositions. Take myself for example; I was a Christian, I believed in a creator because I was taught as much from a very early age. It took years of debates, questions, reading, interpreting, more debate and more questions before I was able to rid myself of the religious baggage. Of course, where ID makes the presupposition that there was a creator, evolution makes no such assumption and instead allows the freethinker to make up his or her own mind.

You say, "without the framework of the Bible and the understanding that evil entered the world through man's actions (*Genesis 3*), God appears sloppy and incompetent", but even with the biblical framework, God appears sloppy. Consider that this planet is not a perfect specimen.

Did god create the Earth to fit life, or did life adapt to fit the conditions of Earth over 4.5 billion years? Well, here's the thing; if any of the conditions that we find ourselves in were different (our distance from the sun and our moon, our elliptical orbit, out rotational axis, the density of our iron core, our rate of spin, our atmospheric density) making it impossible for human life to exist on Earth as it does today, the universe would still exist. Bacteria and some sea life might still exist. In fact, if things were so different, I might be writing this book in a freaking tadpole pad on the bottom of the ocean and I could finally have my way with my own *little mermaid*!

An Anthropomorphized Universe

Human ignorance and Human arrogance has ultimately resulted in an 'Anthropocentric' or what I like to call a 'homocentric' (not associated with the Westboro Baptist Church) view of the universe. That is, that all life and all matter exists for us and because of us. Yet this is clearly not true, humans aren't the focus of the universe, the universe has tried to smash the Earth out of existence on more than one occasion (obviously not with any form of malice though, after all, we owe the presence of our moon – and therefore our tides and axis – to a massive collision about 4.5 billion years ago)!

As awesome as we like to think that we are, the universe was not created for humanity and its whims. There is proof of this in the notion that in the time that you sleep each night, a star in a distant galaxy has erupted into either a neutron star or a black hole. Of course, that factoid was bullshit, but all you have to do to disprove the notion of a universe created for humanity is to look up at the stars. Each one of those twinkly pinpricks is just another of literally hundreds of billions of suns in our Milky Way galaxy, and there are more galaxies than there are Chinese and Mexicans put together. We're talking possibly trillions of trillions of stars.

Put simply, we're nothing. We're less than nothing. On a universal scale, we're infinite times smaller than a bacterial flagellum on the herpes on the vestigial penis of a flea.

If the universe was created for humanity, then what's with all the rest of the planets? What a complete waste of real estate! You think God would have given us some room to spread out. I mean, with the technology He left us with (i.e. sweet nothing), we are stuck on this planet. Our planet, where over 75% of the total mass is water which we can't readily use; and much of the land is just as useless, with desert, rocky mountains, or sub-zero polar regions. Where is the intelligence in that? If the earth is so perfectly designed, then why do we spend billions of dollars every year changing the temperature of our homes?

You and I are what the cosmos can accomplish if given 13.7 billion years.

But you know what they say; God never closes a door without opening a window... which is why the heating bill in Heaven is so God damned expensive!

The very idea that God intelligently designed the universe for us is laughable. Our nearest planet will take a minimum of a few months to travel to (based on current technology) and is not habitable outside of human made structures. Hell, space travel its self presents more danger than traversing a live volcano during an eruption - space is a complete vacuum and it is in a constant state of radiation flux. Any planet that we go to is either too hot or too cold, and we can't even land on the gas giants! Some designer *He* turned out to be! The whole universe created just for us and we get stuck in this tiny little ball of water and dirt!

The Deadbeat Dad/God

Intelligent Design asserts there is a benign creator out there who through thought and will and toil intervened gave birth to this universe and created everything we see and experience today. But such an assertion is simply frightening. Think of it this way, there's a God out there who was powerful enough to create, but doesn't give a crap about the maintenance. Why does this benign God not intervene in child abuse, in genocide or in war? We're talking about the God of the Jews here and the Jews themselves have been through more shit than any other race in recorded history! The holocaust happened and Hitler didn't even get so much as a freaking case of lazy bowel syndrome! Or was the Holocaust just punishment for killing Jesus 2000 years earlier? Bullshit!

"People ask why God is unable to prevent evil from thwarting His plans, resulting in such poor design, instead of understanding that because of the Fall there is now a cursed design," so proclaim-eth the pseudo scientist! Problem with your assertion is that humans were apparently made in God's own image. We are, therefore, perfect, so even if humanity lost its immortality after eating from the Tree of Knowledge, our forms would have remained unchanged, right? So what's with the coccyx? That little bump (vestigial tail) in between the top of your bum crack that has served no purpose since our ancestors were able to balance whilst standing up. What about the appendix? It no longer serves the purpose that it used to (replenishing the gut with beneficial bacteria after it was killed off by a serious case of the mega-volcano-squirts).

We have remnants of our own evolution within our own body. An interesting fact is that in the last 20 years, the number of people with vitamin D deficiency has skyrocketed. So what has happened in the last 20 years for this to happen so rapidly? Well, for the last two decades, we've been told to slip on a shirt, slop on some sunscreen and slap on a hat to prevent skin cancer and melanoma. Problem is that for the last several billion years, our predecessors have been absorbing vitamin D from the sun through their skin. This is a small proof of evolution in our own bodies!

As are the genetic conditions of Cystic Fibrosis and Sickle Cell Anemia. About 50,000 years ago in Europe, Tuberculosis was incredibly prevalent and was killing off half of all children by the age of five and lay waste to entire generations. If a child carried a single mutation (from one parent) in the Cystic Fibrosis Transmembrane Conductance, they produced slightly thicker mucus in their lungs protecting them slightly better than those without the mutation from TB, Cholera and Typhoid. Of course, if the child carried two copies of the gene, they'd develop Cystic Fibrosis and die, and would likely also die without the mutation. This meant that mainly those with the mutation would survive to maturity to reproduce. Evolutionists call this *strong selection*; and genetic mutation that increased the resistance to such a devastating disease would spread quickly (because the rest would be flower manure).

In a very similar way, about 100,000 years ago, a single letter in the gene paragraph, which describes the structure of hemoglobin, changed in one person. This kind of mutation is usually inconsequential, but in this case, it resulted in a new form of hemoglobin

(hemoglobin S) that had the amazing property of being resistant to the parasite Malaria! If a child receives the mutation from one parent, they can resist the parasite. Sickle Cell Anemia, however, is inherited when a child inherits the hemoglobin S mutation from both parents. This child will have a very painful life as abnormally shaped red blood cells get jammed in joints, organs and blood vessels.

As a molecular geneticist, you can 'see' these mutations, Georgia. If we are the product of a designer, why do these mutations exist? I'm left with two options; you're either a complete moron, you a very bad molecular geneticist.

The Logic of the Bible Lover

You mention the resurrection and arrogantly suggest "Jesus clearly conquered death with the Resurrection," (*Romans 6:3–10*) but using the Bible to prove the Bible does not make it true or factual. We already know that the Bible is neither useful as an actual science or historically accurate text book, and we know nothing of Jesus' actual life, just what the apostles wrote about him 50-250 years after Jesus the Jew had died. The fact that THERE IS ABSOLUTELY NOTHING WRITTEN OF JESUS FROM HIS OWN TIME despite there being noted historians in the same place as Jesus at the same time as Jesus kind of leads the sane person to the conclusion that the story of Jesus is to factual as skydiving without a parachute is to safe.

You say that "knowledge of God must come through both general revelation (nature) and special revelation (the Bible)", but this would only be considered a good idea if the Bible were factually correct, which it is not. The creator is an Abrahamic religion's invention, not a fact. Every single civilization that has habituated on this earth has had some form of deity or another. Their claim of deities and their form of worship is no more or less valid than the Judeo-Christian one, yours is just newer... and far more bloodthirsty... what the hell is with that foreskin fetish of his, anyway?

The only reason you believe your God created the universe and everything within, is because of the Roman Emperor Constantine's adoption of Christianity during a major battle (that he coincidentally won after donning the Christian Cross). If that had not happened, Rome would have continued to persecute Christians (feed the crazy bastards to the lions) and worship Jupiter and his kick ass squad of super Gods (which were simply adaptations of the Greek Gods). Christianity spread as Rome conquered nation after nation. If this had never happened the early Christians would have been slaughtered out of existence, Islam wouldn't have been founded and the Jews would have been the only ones worshiping the singular monotheistic God (because I dare not mention Zoroaster).

My point is simple, the assertion of ID is not based on fact; - it is based on religion. Religion is literally, belief IN DIRECT SPITE of contrary evidence, faith IN SPITE of reason. As such it is not scientific, and it holds no credence in a world of evidence based reason and logic.

You purport that Jesus is the Good News, but he is described by the Apostle Paul, and in the Gospels of Matthew, Mark, Luke and John, as a bigot; a racist; a communist; he was mean to his parents; he was anti-establishment; believed in killing children if they talked back to their parents; his parents and apostles remarked several times that they thought he was mentally ill; and was an all around asshole. Jesus was not prophetic, he was not prolific; he was an apocalyptic preacher and ultimately pathetic. If we are to take anything from the New Testament, it is that Jesus challenged the status quo and was killed for being too much of a radical punk-ass. He was a fool, and he was killed for it.

Ultimately, Georgia, you've left me completely underwhelmed with your creationist and intelligent design claims. The resources you claim to have produced are nothing more than assertions based, convoluted strings of convoluted logic and assumptions that the Bible is a reliable source of factual information, which any reputable historian will tell you that it is not.

You appear deluded and you aim to share your delusion with the next generation of stupid, blind and ignorant Christian idiots. You give them all the proof they need to claim piety and retard their intellectual capacity to ensure that they do nothing of use to society in the professional years, only to spread the ignorance onto further generations. If only you lived up to your qualifications, Georgia, if only.

May Thundercat have mercy on your soul (a soul which your God created on command from Thundercat) - Praise be to Thundercat!

Irreducibly yours,

Jake Farr-Wharton

Hitler and Stalin Were Atheists, So All Atheists Are Evil

Dinesh D'Souza is the Rishwain Fellow at the Hoover Institution. His latest book is *The Enemy at Home: The Cultural Left and Its Responsibility for 9/11.* D'Souza is a noted defender of Christianity and conservative writer and speaker. He is the author of numerous New York Times best-selling books. He was born and raised Catholic, but now considers himself an Evangelical Christian. Here's an excerpt from *"Atheism, not religion, is the real force behind the mass murders of history"* by Dinesh D'Souza...

In recent months, a spate of atheist books have argued that religion represents, as "End of Faith" author Sam Harris puts it, "the most potent source of human conflict, past and present."

Columnist Robert Kuttner gives the familiar litany. "The Crusades slaughtered millions in the name of Jesus. The Inquisition brought the torture and murder of millions more. After Martin Luther, Christians did bloody battle with other Christians for another three centuries."

In his bestseller "The God Delusion," Richard Dawkins contends that most of the world's recent conflicts – in the Middle East, in the Balkans, in Northern Ireland, in Kashmir, and in Sri Lanka – show the vitality of religion's murderous impulse.

The problem with this critique is that it exaggerates the crimes attributed to religion, while ignoring the greater crimes of secular fanaticism. The best example of religious persecution in America is the Salem witch trials. How many people were killed in those trials? Thousands? Hundreds? Actually, fewer than 25. Yet the event still haunts the liberal imagination.

It is strange to witness the passion with which some secular figures rail against the misdeeds of the Crusaders and Inquisitors more than 500 years ago. The number sentenced to death by the Spanish Inquisition appears to be about 10,000. Some historians contend that an additional 100,000 died in jail due to malnutrition or illness.

These figures are tragic, and of course population levels were much lower at the time. But even so, they are minuscule compared with the death tolls produced by the atheist despotisms of the 20th century. In the name of creating their version of a religion-free utopia, Adolf Hitler, Joseph Stalin, and Mao Zedong produced the kind of mass slaughter that no Inquisitor could possibly match. Collectively these atheist tyrants murdered more than 100 million people.

Moreover, many of the conflicts that are counted as "religious wars" were not fought over religion. They were mainly fought over rival claims to territory and power. Can the wars between England and France be called religious wars because the English were Protestants and the French were Catholics? Hardly.

The same is true today. The Israeli-Palestinian conflict is not, at its core, a religious one. It arises out of a dispute over self-determination and land. Hamas and the extreme orthodox parties in Israel may advance theological claims – "God gave us this land" and so forth – but the conflict would remain essentially the same even without these religious motives. Ethnic rivalry, not religion, is the source of the tension in Northern Ireland and the Balkans.

Yet today's atheists insist on making religion the culprit. Consider Mr. Harris's analysis of the conflict in Sri Lanka. "While the motivations of the Tamil Tigers are not explicitly religious," he informs us, "they are Hindus who undoubtedly believe many improbable things about the nature of life and death." In other words, while the Tigers see themselves as combatants in a secular political struggle, Harris detects a religious motive because these people happen to be Hindu and surely there must be some underlying religious craziness that explains their fanaticism.

Harris can go on forever in this vein. Seeking to exonerate secularism and atheism from the horrors perpetrated in their name, he argues that Stalinism and Maoism were in reality "little more than a political religion." As for Nazism, "while the hatred of Jews in Germany expressed itself in a predominantly secular way, it was a direct inheritance from medieval Christianity." Indeed, "The holocaust marked the culmination of ... two thousand years of Christian fulminating against the Jews."

One finds the same inanities in Mr. Dawkins's work. Don't be fooled by this rhetorical legerdemain. Dawkins and Harris cannot explain why, if Nazism was directly descended from medieval Christianity, medieval Christianity did not produce a Hitler. How can a self-proclaimed atheist ideology, advanced by Hitler as a repudiation of Christianity, be a "culmination" of 2,000 years of Christianity? Dawkins and Harris are employing a transparent sleight of hand that holds Christianity responsible for the crimes committed in its name, while exonerating secularism and atheism for the greater crimes committed in their name.

Religious fanatics have done things that are impossible to defend, and some of them, mostly in the Muslim world, are still performing horrors in the name of their creed. But if religion sometimes disposes people to self-righteousness and absolutism, it also provides a moral code that condemns the slaughter of innocents. In particular, the moral teachings of Jesus provide no support for – indeed they stand as a stern rebuke to – the historical injustices perpetrated in the name of Christianity.

The crimes of atheism have generally been perpetrated through a hubristic ideology that sees man, not God, as the creator of values. Using the latest techniques of science and technology, man seeks to displace God and create a secular utopia here on Earth. Of course if some people – the Jews, the landowners, the unfit, or the handicapped – have to be eliminated in order to achieve this utopia, this is a price the atheist tyrants and their apologists have shown themselves quite willing to pay. Thus they confirm the truth of Fyodor Dostoyevsky's dictum, "If God is not, everything is permitted."

Whatever the motives for atheist bloodthirstiness, the indisputable fact is that all the religions of the world put together have in 2,000 years not managed to kill as many people as have been killed in the name of atheism in the past few decades.

It's time to abandon the mindlessly repeated mantra that religious belief has been the greatest source of human conflict and violence. Atheism, not religion, is the real force behind the mass murders of history.

Dear Dinesh,

One of the most pleasant facets associated with being an outspoken, loud and proud atheist is the contemptuous emails and letters one is bound to receive. I frequently receive, what I call, 'Justification Emails' whereby the Christian author is attempting to refute my assertion that biblical morality is a joke by claiming that if they "didn't have the fear of God driving their actions, they'd go on a shooting spree." I'll say the same thing to you that I do to them:

If the only thing preventing you from murdering, raping, torturing, molesting or any other atrocity you can think of is 'the fear of god's wrath', then please, PLEASE, get yourself to the nearest mental health facility!

Checkmate

In all seriousness, Dinesh, it has gone beyond the stage of annoyance towards the insinuation theists make that atheism is evil because Hitler and Stalin were atheists. It is a completely unfounded assertion!

Theists constantly retreat to it in a last-ditched attempt at misdirection, when the subject of religion directly causing and inspiring incalculable atrocities around the globe since the invention of gods is raised. It is a most certainly a false assertion, and one that has been put to rest by historians ad infinitum. But you Christians keep marching it out in the hope that if you say it enough times, we will forget what really did take place in the middle of the 20th century.

Firstly, I have to take a moment to laugh at your claim that, "The number sentenced to death by the Spanish Inquisition appears to be about 10,000". I read this and thought where on earth did you come up with this astoundingly low number? So I put on my detectives hat, had a toke on my Sherlock Holmes pipe (tobacco, I swear!) - only for the fact that I love getting into character when I am hell bent on assassinating an opportunistic evangelical's character – and found your source.

With a little old fashioned investigative journalism, I discovered that you found, literally, the lowest estimate for the total number of people savagely (savage is an understatement) tortured in the days and hours before their horrific deaths. You got your figure from the Vatican, you sneaky little devil, you. The Vatican (Pope Gregory) ordered the slaughter, and you took the number of slaughtered from the accounts of the perpetrators. Somewhat the equivalent of believing the Nazi account that just a few Jews were hurt in

Auschwitz due to falling down a flight of stairs, "not our fault that a gas chamber was at the bottom of it"… I hate to tell you, Dinesh, but your source is about as reliable as asking a heroin addict to hold onto your cash filled wallet while you paddle out for a surf!

In fact, your source was a 2004 report compiled by a Catholic historian at the Sapienza University in Rome. Hardly an independent, impartial report is it, Dinesh? Certainly, a long way off the range, estimated by a large number of historians, to be in the hundreds of thousands, possibly millions. These 'heretics' spent their final hours burning on a stake; impaled through the anus by rotating rods; women pierced in half with entrance through their genitalia; all of this unimaginable horror performed as per the decree of the Vatican.

Why? They were accused of being non-believers of Jesus Christ, or falsely accused of witchcraft or sorcery. And you don't think the Vatican sponsored study from a Vatican academic has a self-interest in declaring such an outrageously low number? This is as "fair and balanced" as a Fox News report on public support for Barack Obama.

That said, I'm not going to argue over the number slain by Papal order during the Inquisition. I would, however, like to make the point that theists, and I feel compelled to lump you in with them, fictionalize the facts in order to defend or promote your faith. With seemingly malicious cleverness, you make reference to the Crusades but no mention of the 9 million killed in God's name during that particular Jesus inspired campaign. It's this kind of intellectual dishonesty that Christians, who again I feel compelled to place you with, are infamous for (and what we atheists have ultimately come to expect from people like you). When arbitrary claims, contrary to historical evidence, are made by parties with a strong vested interest, they need to be called out. Consider this as me calling you out.

Atheist Despots

The hallmarks of your disingenuous article continue where you write; "they (the number killed by religious violence) are minuscule compared with the death tolls produced by the atheist despotisms of the 20th century." WTF? Atheist despots? I've heard the term Nazi despot, Communist despot, maniacal despot, and religious despot, but an "atheist despot"?

Are you suggesting Stalin killed millions of people in the name of 'lack of belief in gods'? Who, in fact, commits any moral atrocity in the name of atheism? Who kills, rapes, or tortures in the name of what is literally 'lack of belief in gods and the supernatural'?

Unlike Christianity, Islam and Judaism, there is no atheist doctrine that exists to justify such action, simple as that! It's like saying Stalin killed in the name of not believing in Santa Claus. Or Hitler killed 6 million Jews because he didn't really believe Thor carried a hammer. Or, equally absurd, Hitler and Stalin killed millions of innocents because they both had mustaches. Your claim takes ridiculousness to a new level!

Your assertions are not only misleading, but they are flat out fallacious. The fallacy that applies here is called "correlation does not prove causation". In other words, that two things that happen together does not prove they are related, non-sequiturs. Hitler and Stalin being atheists does not prove that atheists are evil – if it did, we could also say that both of these men had mustaches, and all men with mustaches are evil! I personally take exception to that, Dinesh, I have a stunning mustache, and have not killed a single Russian or Jew! That, by the way, does not for a second mean that I concede your assertion that Hitler or Stalin were, in fact, atheists. Let us examine Hitler first. What did he have to say?

> *"My feelings as a Christian point me to my Lord and Savior as a fighter. It points me to the man who once in loneliness, surrounded by a few followers, recognized these Jews for what they were and summoned men to fight against them and who, God's truth! was greatest not as a sufferer but as a fighter. In boundless love as a Christian and as a man I read through the passage which tells us how the Lord at last rose in His might and seized the scourge to drive out of the Temple the brood of vipers and adders. How terrific was His fight for the world against the Jewish poison. To-day, after two thousand years, with deepest emotion I recognize more profoundly than ever before the fact that it was for this that He had to shed His blood upon the Cross. As a Christian I have no duty to allow myself to be cheated, but I have the duty to be a fighter for truth and justice… And if there is anything which could demonstrate that we are acting rightly it is the distress that daily grows. For as a Christian I have also a duty to my own people."*

Wow! Hitler was a Christian? I had no idea! Ha, ha, I totally *did* know he was a Christian; I was just lying for effect. So how is it that I know, and you don't know? I mean, this information is available on the internet, in books, in documentaries, in tattoos on the chests of American Nazis and Skin Heads, it's not as though you'd have to dig very deep… certainly not as deep as you would have had to have dug, so as to arrive at your number of 10,000 slaughtered on Catholic decree. Still not convinced?

"I am now as before a Catholic and will always remain so." (Adolf Hitler, to Gen. Gerhard Engel, 1941)

Moreover, he was raised in a Roman Catholic household, and there is no reason to suggest that he ever abandoned the faith of the kiddy fiddlers – abstinence does indeed make the church grow fondlers! In fact his autobiography, *Mein Kampf*, is littered with black and white declarations of his Catholicism. And you mustn't forget that he used Jesus as a tool to convince not only himself but also the majority of Lutherans and Catholics in Germany that killing Jews would please the Almighty:

"I believe that I am acting in accordance with the will of the Almighty Creator: by defending myself against the Jew, I am fighting for the work of the Lord." (Adolf Hitler)

While Hitler was not among the regular Sunday churchgoers, and later criticized the Church for their rejection of his reformation of a unified German Church, but at no time did Hitler criticize the malevolent cosmic duo of the Big Man or JC. He always maintained an honor and belief in Jesus. Face it, Hitler was one of the flock… he was a devout Christian believer. But Hitler's religiosity didn't just start and finish there; he devoted his entire political life to deeds aimed at creating a race of people in the pure image of God. This Nazism ideology is absolutely indistinguishable from a religious ideology.

As such, any attempt to paint atheism as evil is nothing more than desperation personified as inaccurate misdirection. It is an attempt to put an evil face to non-belief in the same way that Pope Eggs Benedict is the head of pedophilia cover-ups. You aim to shame people into adopting Christianity as a way to save their soul from the 'same moral destitution' that ensnared Stalin and Hitler. But as you can see we are well on the way to proving Hitler was anything but an atheist. Further, before you go play the 'Hitler didn't behave like a Christian' card, why don't you take a moment to compare his rhetoric, as illustrated earlier, with the language that Pope Urban II used to ignite the flames of anti-Semitic hatred when he called for the Crusades:

> "...hasten to exterminate this vile race from the lands of your brethren, Christ commands it. And if those who set out thither should lose their lives on the way by land, or in crossing the sea, or in fighting the pagans, their sins shall be remitted. Oh what a disgrace, if a race so despised, base, and the instrument of demons, should so overcome a people endowed with faith in the all-powerful God, and resplendent with the name of Christ." (Pope Urban II

Furthermore, the Holocaust had its roots in the Christian anti-Semitism, as Sam Harris pointed out, that never entirely left Europe after the conclusion of the Crusades. The Jews burdened with a 'Blood Libel', the murderers of Jesus, were blamed for every ill Europe ever suffered. "Oh shit, we're all dying from the plague. It's the evil Jews! Let's burn them." Thus Hitler was able to tap into the indictment of Medieval Christianity against the Jews to take wind up the machinery of hate. Propaganda is a wonderful, fruitful, maddening thing!

Obama is Hitler

Did Hitler lie when he promoted religion, instead using it for political gain?

It would be certainly understandable that Hitler would do such a thing; after all, most of history's despots have used some form of ideology to inspire support and justify their actions. But here's 'the thing'; nothing in the historical record indicates this of Hitler.

Even if he lied in *Mein Kampf,* why would he continue to consider himself a Christian after he held absolute German power? Why expend so many valuable resources just to rid Germany of Jews if not from some profound justification? Sure they have possibly the greatest squiggly side burns of all time and a more attractive appendage; but not even prettier penis envy would explain Hitler's all consuming dread towards the Jews. The hate must stem from some source and the historical record shows that anti-Judaism had long lived in the minds of Christians ever since Paul had his hunger-induced deliriums (it's in the Bible, look it up) and decided he'd throw his lot in with Jesus instead of the Jews (which is ridiculous considering that Jesus was an orthodox Jew).

Furthermore, what the hell is with you Christian conservatives likening everything that upsets your status quo to Hitler? You've got the strangest form of obsessive-compulsive disorder that I ever did see! "Obama is Hitler", "Gore is Hitler", "Saddam was Hitler", and yet Bush, Christine O'Donnell, Rand Paul and Sarah Palin are sexy, freaking angels wrapped in pretty tinsel?

Enough! Find another despot to relate all the evil in the world to, or at least sound a wee bit smarter than your two-time B… B… Bush voting track record would have us believe. Mind you, Bush, the evangelical Christian, was a pretty thorough President; when he left the presidency, he left the country thoroughly in debt with no hope for quick return; America and several other 'coalition' countries thoroughly engaged in a war that should never have been started and the majority of Americans thoroughly disenfranchised with their nation and electoral system. I digress.

The Nazis wore the slogan, "Got mit uns" (God's with us) on their belt buckles. Even if Hitler was an atheist, and there is really no evidence to support that he was atheist, his soldiers were Lutheran observing Christians. Ultimately, the beliefs of the Nazis were a direct descendent of medieval anti-Semitism that ran unchecked in Europe which originated during the period of the Christian Crusades.

Ok, so let me never hear you mention Hitler's name again when arguing for the demons of atheism. I will smack that argument down so hard that Whitney Houston will reconsider Bobby Brown a tender lover!

The Endorsement of the Russian Orthodox Church
Now, let us look at Stalin. Well, firstly Stalin was anti-religious rather than atheist. There is a big difference there. First of all, Stalin was schooled in a seminary, and whilst yes he publicly renounced his faith, he was ultimately, like Hitler, a dictator who ruled by his own ideology. One cannot be in the dictator business without using the social machinery in place to leverage your power. As such, he used the Orthodox Church and had

their public blessing as having been *chosen by God* to lead his people.

Basically, he used the church for what it had originally been intended, to impose control on the gullible populace.

A quick glance of the *Dummies Guide to Dictatorship* will show you that the first rule of Dictator's club is to construct a cult of personality. It's difficult to get the people to bow down and chant, "All Hail Stalin", when they are in Church on Sundays praising Jesus. There can only ever be one true god, and for Stalin he had to be just that. Once you're *the man* you can do whatever you like to your opposition. Usually, exile or kill them. Which Stalin most certainly did!

Stalin was uber successful in establishing that kind of god-like cult status. In a 1956 speech, Nikita Khrushchev gave a denunciation of Stalin's actions:

"It is impermissible and foreign to the spirit of
Marxism-Leninism to elevate one person, to transform
him into a superman possessing supernatural
characteristics akin to those of a god."

Stalin used all the tasty carrots of the supernatural such as miracles – the promise of miraculously fruitful harvest, which invariably led to famine. Ultimately, Stalin's regime was merely about power, not about unbelief. He used a pseudo-religion or quasi-religious ideology, not atheism. He needed the people to believe that he *was* God! Whilst Stalin may have been an atheist in his middle years, he was not especially rational.

The problem with Stalin and his contemporaries has nothing to do with their rejection of religious belief, and just about everything to do with THE FACT THAT THEY'RE COMPLETELY DELUDED TOTALITARIAN PSYCHOPATHS. They entice (enforce) blind faith (servitude) and are completely unable to come through with their promises.

Kim Jong-Il, for example, has the North Koreans believing that his father was God, and that he is the reincarnation of his father. In this sense, North Korea is just one ghost short of a trinity. Hey, have you ever noticed that Kim Jong-Il looks like Yoda and Pope Benedict looks like The Emperor from Star Wars (after the lightning to the face)? I think George Lucas was onto something!

Killing In The Name Of...

It is simply illogical and unreasonable to make the charge that these lunatic despots killed in the name of unbelief. It is equally irrational to assert that atheism is the cause for their behavior. They are inhuman, psychopathic, totalitarians.

If you want to prove your point, you'd need to set up two separate bio-dome experiments, each one with a hundred or so babies and their parents. In one, you feed the children Christian doctrine as they grow, and in the other you feed them logic, reasoning and empathy. While such a hypothetical is ultimately outrageous, invariably, In my opinion, the group which regard life as the only opportunity to experience, is more likely to be far more centered towards altruism over those believing that life is just an intermediate state.

In America, an entire generation of fundamentalist Christians and Evangelicals vehemently believe that

Jesus will come down to enact the rapture within their lifetimes. Both Sarah Palin and John McCain made those assertions during their 2008 presidential campaign. How much value can you put on life if you ultimately believe that it is frugal, fickle and that you will be immortal only once you die?

Atheism doesn't have a written doctrine as a component of its lack of belief, there is never justification for murder, nor rape, nor torture of any form. On the other hand, the Bible, Torah and Koran both justify and urge believers to get up from the sofa and burn a non-believer, homosexual, apostate at the stake:

> "If your very own brother, or your son or daughter, or the wife you love, or your closest friend secretly entices you, saying, 'Let's go out and worship other gods', do not yield to him or listen to him. Show him no pity. Do not spare him or shield him. You must certainly put him to death. Your hand must be the first in putting him to death and then the hands of the people. Stone him to death because he tried to turn you away from the Lord your God…Then all Israel will hear and be afraid, and no-one among you will do such an evil thing again." (Deuteronomy 13:6-11 NIV)

> "Believers, if you yield to the infidels they will drag you back to unbelief and you will return headlong to perdition. We will put terror into the hearts of the unbelievers. The fire shall be their home." (Koran 3:149-51)

> "Prophet, make war on the unbelievers and the hypocrites and deal rigorously with them. Hell shall be their home: an evil fate." (Koran 9:73)

The only words in the atheist's Bible are "SHOW ME THE FREAKING EVIDENCE BEFORE I GET ON MY KNEES AND LET THIS PRIEST VIOLATE MY ANUS!"

Dinesh, the way that you've played down the examples of religious violence in centuries past is a deliberately mischievous attempt to water down the confronting reality of the sectarian atrocities. We don't even need to go back decades, we can look at more recent troubles including the still current Palestine vs Israel (Jews vs Muslims); the Balkans (Serbs vs Muslims); Kashmir (Muslims vs Hindus); Sudan (Muslims vs Christians); Nigeria (Muslims vs Christians); Northern Ireland (Protestants vs Catholics); Iraq (Shia vs Shite); Philippines (Muslims vs Christians); Sri Lanka (Sinhalese Budhists vs Tamil Hindus); and the Caucasus (Orthodox Russians vs Chechen Muslims); Cartoonist in Denmark vs Entirety of Islam. You are delusional if you think that turning off your TV at night when all of the above religious genocides are shown on the news is enough to delude yourself into thinking that with atheism we get Hitler and Stalin!

This ridiculous notion that, "if religion sometimes disposes people to self-righteousness and absolutism, it also provides a moral code that condemns the slaughter of innocents. In particular, the moral teachings of Jesus provide no support for – indeed they stand as a stern rebuke to – the historical injustices perpetrated in the name of Christianity", is simply an illustration of your biblical illiteracy. What separates Jesus from other ancient teachers, such as Buddha or Socrates, is that Buddha nor Socrates never proclaimed, "You better listen and obey everything I have to say or the fires of Hell will scorch your genitalia forever, and a day." It was Socrates that first said, "Do unto others as you'd like done to you". As a matter of fact, he said that almost 600 years before Jesus did but he, unlike Jesus, never added a sub-text that read, "or rot in pain for all eternity, you pig face scum". I'm paraphrasing of course, but you get my point.

> *"[Jesus said] Do not think that I came to bring peace on the earth; I did not come to bring peace, but a sword. For I came to set a man against his father, and a daughter against her mother, and a daughter-in-law against her mother-in-law; and a man's enemies will be the members of his household. He who loves father or mother more than Me is not worthy of Me; and he who loves son or daughter more than Me is not worthy of Me. And he who does not take his cross and follow after Me is not worthy of Me. He who has found his life will lose it, and he who has lost his life for My sake will find it." (Matthew 10:34-39)*

Or what of this old chestnut?

> *"And if your eye causes you to sin, pluck it out. It is better for you to enter the kingdom of God with one eye than to have two eyes and be thrown into hell, where 'their worm does not die, and the fire is not quenched'." (Mark 9:47-4)*

To suggest that Jesus did not promote in/out thinking is dishonest of you. He fostered belief that there are *truth* believers and *truth* deniers, and Hell will be the home for the latter... who are evil (which is a fallacy)... but ridiculously handsome (which is true). Rhetoric like this only serves to dehumanize the *many* opponents of your faith, and once you view your theological opponent as sub-human then the perpetration of violent atrocity is made easy (this is how Hitler did it, after all). As such, I feel the need to ask if you were indeed attempting to soften Christianity up for another Holy War... are you?

Just because you included Sam Harris in your article, I will finish with his likewise underscoring my point:

> *"A glance at history, or at the pages of any newspaper, reveals that ideas which divide one group of human beings from another, only to unite them in slaughter, generally have their roots in religion. It seems that if our species ever eradicates itself through war, it will not be because it was written in the stars but because it was written in our books; it is what we do with words like "God" and "paradise" and "afterlife" in the present that will determine our future"* (Sam Harris, End of Faith)

Remember Dinesh, there was a time in Western history when religion ruled the roost; it's well known, you might have heard of it before - the Dark Ages.

Warm regards,

Jake Farr-Wharton

My Karma Ran
Over My Dogma

Dear Reader, the following is an address from the Prelate of Opus Dei, Monsignor Javier Echevarria. He holds doctorates in both civil and canon law. He is the author of books of spirituality such as "Memoria del beato Josemaria," "Itinerarios de vida cristiana," "Para servir a la Iglesia," "Getsemani" and "Eucaristia y vida cristiana." Opus Dei, besides being featured in the horribly inaccurate, but entertaining, novel by Dan Brown, The DaVinci Code, has around 87,000 members worldwide. His full address can be found here: *www.opusdei.us/art.php?p=36702*.

My dear children: may Jesus watch over my daughters and sons for me!

Mary always leads us to Jesus, as happened with those figures from the Orient, the Wise Men, who followed a star to Bethlehem to adore the newborn Messiah. And where did they find him?

On the Solemnity of Mary the Mother of God, our soul is filled with admiration and joy, as we address our Lady with this invocation, the root of all the graces with which our All-powerful God has enriched the one whom, from all eternity, he chose as the Mother of his Son according to human nature. "Because of it, she was conceived immaculate and is full of grace; because of it, she is ever virgin, she was taken up body and soul to Heaven and has been crowned Queen of all creation, above the angels and saints. Greater than she, none but God." All of this is God's will, as the Church teaches and as we Christians believe. "There is no danger of exaggerating," St. Josemaría insists. "We can never hope to fathom this inexpressible mystery; nor will we ever be able to give sufficient thanks to our Mother for bringing us into such intimacy with the Blessed Trinity."

Everything depends on God's grace; and, at the same time, everything depends on the correspondence of Christ's followers, who have to continue the furrow opened by our Lord and deepened by successive generations of the faithful, from the Apostles and the women of the first hour up to today. Doesn't it fill you with joy to consider that our Lord is counting on each and every one of us, despite our personal weaknesses, to proclaim the Gospel to the ends of the earth?

Today there is an urgent need to spread Christ's doctrine, especially in certain sectors. I am thinking above all of those in government, of scientists and researchers, of people working in the field of public opinion, etc. But all of us need to listen to God's voice and follow it. Therefore we should beseech God, with humility, with insistence, with confidence, that he open minds and hearts to his light.

This is the task of all Christians who want to be consistent with their vocation: to show Christ to others, to be a "loudspeaker"— first by their example, but also by their opportune words—of the Church's teachings, especially in the topics most under debate in public opinion: respect for human life in all its phases; the duty of trying to ensure that civil laws foster and protect the true nature of the family established by the Creator, based on the indissoluble marriage of a man and a woman, open to life; the right to chose an educational format for one's children that corresponds to each one's spiritual and moral ideals, etc.

We should consider carefully, in our examination of conscience, how we have helped souls to get closer to God: how much prayer, how much sacrifice, how many hours of well-done work we have offered, how many conversations we have had—personally, or in writing, making use of all the means within our reach—with friends, relatives, colleagues, acquaintances. And we should speak about this holy concern in personal spiritual direction, so that we can be helped and encouraged in the apostolate, which is the duty of every Christian.

All we need to do is look at Jesus Christ, our model at all times. His example leads us to say, yes, it is possible to pray when one knows how to distinguish between the crime and its perpetrator. When we pray for those who kill so savagely, we don't deny the evil of their deeds nor the need to bring them to judgment before the law. There is no justification for evil. Violence is indefensible. But intransigence with evil is surely compatible with something that goes to the heart of the Church's mission—pardoning sinners. Justice is not in conflict with mercy.

Every woman who is in that situation is aware of how she is pulled home: to attend a sick child, to keep up with the multitude of tasks a home generates, not to speak of pregnancy and maternity. Other times it is the outside job that pulls on her, because the income is necessary for the family's advancement; or because every enterprise demands results, not always in a reasonable or flexible way; or because of the need for professional competence and the threat of unemployment.

On the path of feminism I see traces of the sexual revolution and the fear of having more children that divert the liberation of women from its true ends. This is very different from forms of feminism—usually aggressive—that treat sex as anthropologically and socially irrelevant, as something purely physiological. Taking seriously the dignity of women has to spread first of all among women themselves by eradicating all forms of inferiority complex. This requires calling things by their names and rejecting, for example, everything that is conducive to the shameful business of pornography; the sad and mistaken affirmation of a "right" to abortion; the social disgrace—also deeply offensive to God—of divorce.

Dear Javier,

First up, I'd like to make it clear that the reason I will address you by your first name is directly related to my distinct lack of respect for Catholicism, my disdain for inferred piety and my complete lack of reverence for the hierarchy of the Catholic Church and its many spinoff sects and cults.

To refer to you as 'father' would distort the very meaning of the word 'father' and would ultimately demean the love, respect and reverence I have for my own father, which is in deep contrast to the disdain I hold for you, as the head of Opus Dei and of the upper echelons of Catholicism.

I consider myself one of the lucky ones who, after having left Catholicism, was able to deprogram the very real disease of 'Catholic Guilt' (it's in the frigging dictionary) and 'Sin' which the Catholic Church imbues in each and every boy and girl indoctrinated into your utterly delusional and morally repugnant belief system.

Now that we've got that all cleared up, I'd say it's time for some fun, yeah?

The Dogma Delusion

I note that you start many of your addresses with, "My dear children: may Jesus watch over my daughters and sons for me!" but I, as a rational person, find this somewhat oxymoronic, considering your vow of celibacy. Your assumed piety and inferred 'holiness' ensures that the hearts and minds of many are enrapt by your disgusting dogma of fear, intolerance, segregation and bigotry.

The Catholic church, and by extension, its lawyered and cashed up arm, Opus Dei, is directly responsible for a great many terrors throughout recorded history. From the Crusades, to the Inquisition, to the slaughter of the Templar's, to the imprisonment and ridicule of men of science, the church has a great deal to answer for. More recently, the genocide of the native Tutsi and Hutu people of Rwanda and we should never forget that your abhorrent doctrine of blood, sin and Anti-Semitism gave motive to Hitler:

> *Hence today I believe that I am acting in accordance with the will of the Almighty Creator: by defending myself against the Jew, I am fighting for the work of the Lord (Mein Kampf p. 60)*

Hitler's sentiments are backed up by the bastard father of Catholicism, your very own St Paul:

> *And whatsoever ye do in word or deed, do all in the name of the Lord Jesus, giving thanks to God and the Father by him. (Colossians 3:17)*

About five million Jewish people died in the name of your God, Jesus and your hateful scriptures. Even more recently, you only need to look to Africa to see the Catholic Church's good deeds in practice. In a continent where AIDs, HIV and many other serious communicable diseases run supremely rampant, the message from the clinically despotic Pope Eggs Benedict is, "condoms are an abomination; so just don't have sex". I mean, it is one thing to be naive and yet another to be so maliciously ignorant as to ensure the spread of diseases which can now be prevented.

Kevin Dowling, a South African Catholic Bishop has this to say of the people of Africa:

"Abstinence before marriage and fidelity within a marriage are out of the question here. The issue at hand is to protect life. And that should be our main goal. They have to wear condoms and that's it."

The Church has a social responsibility to protect its followers from harm, and instead of promoting the use of condoms, a practice that, if adhered to, would STOP THE SPREAD OF AIDs (and several other diseases prevalent in Africa), they actively promote a completely fabricated 'evil' of condoms. These are simple, uneducated people, they hear and they believe, just as you and your church taught them to. By promoting the supposed and completely unfounded evil of condoms, Catholicism is not being part of the solution, no; it is maliciously and viciously ensuring that the problem will continue for generations to come.

These priests, and by extension you, don't sound like anyone that any person should refer to as 'father' and considering the atrocities you and your church have perpetrated, I would rather dive into a pool filled with rusty razor blades than be referred to as one of your sons or daughters.

I would suggest you start beginning all of your addresses with, "Jesus, take a break from World of Warcraft, get off your couch-potato ass and actually do something... anything; it's getting hard to convince people that you can circumvent natural laws when you've not done any-bloody-thing since telling your disciples you'd return to take them to Heaven within their lifetimes, 2,000 years ago..."

The Birth of Bullshit

Now, on the birth of Jesus, the birth of Christ appears in only two of the four Gospels chronicling Jesus' life, Matthew and Luke. Mark, author of the first Gospel written c.75 years after Jesus' death completely omitted his birth. The various Christian sects and cults have always revered the story of Jesus' birth, so it is pretty significant that Mark didn't write of the fanciful virgin birth, or the 'three wise men' or that he was a God in the Flesh. Mark, the only gospel author who wrote of Jesus within one or two generations of his death, and he writes nothing of the fantasy surrounding the virgin birth, the three wise men or the fact that he was in fact God. Why do you suppose that is?

The earliest texts, those by the Apostle Paul, don't refer to Jesus' virgin birth either. Paul says that Jesus *"was born of the seed of David" (Romans 1:3)* and was *"born of a woman,"* i.e. not a virgin *(Galatians 4:4)*. The rest of Paul's musings referred to Jesus in an almost completely ethereal sense, as though he were from Heaven, not ever having been of flesh.

In case you were unaware Javier, Jesus' birth was required to convince skeptical Jews that Jesus had fulfilled Old Testament prophesy, and as such, was the messiah.

Unfortunately, the authors of Matthew and Luke didn't get their stories or historical data straight. Thus, it is quite appropriate to discount the silly notions that 'wise men', 'wise kings', "magi' or 'kings of the orient' cared one iota about the little baby Jesus, and so why should anybody else? Why place such significance on something that is so easily refuted as an embellished and make-believe story?

So, why such veneration and admiration for Mary? If Paul, the author of the earliest texts on Jesus' new fabulous laws, didn't consider Mary any more than a lover of fine Jewish sausage (possibly also missionary position lover?) then why should anyone else? If Mark, the author of the first Gospel omitted the notion of Jesus being born of a virgin and being the incarnation of God, then why should anyone else? There is a reason why hearsay is inadmissible in a court of law... it's because it is most likely bullshit!

The Gospels that do install the virgin birth and the God of the flesh myth came much later and are clearly fabricated. Hey, but at least you get to wear those pretty dresses and hats, right?

Choosing the Virgin

With regards to your claims of an 'all-powerful God' choosing a mother for his son, this seems to be the one and only thing that God has done in several millennia. After all, before the Christians claimed your God, He was the God of the Jews, and He clearly couldn't have cared less about their plight during the crusades, the inquisition and the Holocaust. Seriously, about six million of God's chosen people were exterminated, and Hitler didn't even get so much as a speech impediment!

All over the world, natural disasters kill thousands of people, acts of terror in the name of your God occur daily in the Middle East regularly killing tens, if not hundreds, this stuff happens, right? Well, if your God is all-powerful, then He could have easily prevented all such atrocities by simply exerting his will, but he doesn't.

If you want to play the apologetic card and say that it was simply 'these people's' time, then what about the cases of children born with terminal illness such as AIDs or Down's Syndrome? Many of these babies live very short lives in excruciating pain, what bloody purpose does this serve?

God shot some hot Holy Spirit all over Mary and impregnated her; ergo, he can obviously circumvent the laws of nature by exerting his will. As such, it wouldn't be all that much to expect that an all-powerful God would alter the genes of babies whilst still in the womb, so as to ensure that they're born without any defects and are able to live long and healthy lives... hell, they might even have the chance to grow up to inspire humanity to worship your magical sky pixie.

The Immaculate Conception is a curious matter indeed. The Church has done everything in its power to make the conception seem wonderful and fantastic, because it resulted in the birth of Jesus. As a result, Christmas is celebrated every year by Christians all over the world. Problem is, Christmas is nothing more than a celebration of the nine-month anniversary of Mary's rape. Feminists, take heed:

"In the sixth month, God sent the angel Gabriel to Nazareth, a town in Galilee, to a virgin pledged to be married to a man named Joseph, a descendant of David. The virgin's name was Mary. The angel went to her and said, "Greetings, you who are highly favored! The Lord is with you."

Mary was greatly troubled at his words and wondered what kind of greeting this might be. But the angel said to her, "Do not be afraid, Mary, you have found favor with God. You will be with child and give birth to a son, and you are to give him the name Jesus. He will be great and will be called the Son of the Most High. The

137

> *Lord God will give him the throne of his father David,*
> *and he will reign over the house of Jacob forever; his*
> *kingdom will never end."*
>
> *"How will this be," Mary asked the angel, "since I am*
> *a virgin?"*
>
> *The angel answered, "The Holy Spirit will come upon*
> *you, and the power of the Most High will overshadow*
> *you. So the holy one to be born will be called the Son of*
> *God." (Luke 1:26-36 NIV)*

"The Holy Spirit will come upon you". Evocative language, but invariably it describes that Mary had no choice in the matter.

So if the so-called 'Immaculate Conception' was an extension of 'God's will', then the ability to impregnate women somewhat arbitrarily seems to be his only power. St. Josemaría insists that there is no danger in exaggerating, but I would beg to differ. You see, if it were discovered that Jesus were no more than an evangelical Jewish Rabbi of his time, and all of the rest, immaculate conception, being the 'son of God', the miracles, the healing, the resurrection, then the entirety of Christianity would be better described as an exaggeration. Why would I question the story of Jesus' life?

The Jesus Myth

The story of supernatural aspects of Jesus' life, as told by the apostles, simply isn't original. His and the story of Horus, the Egyptian Sun God are virtually identical:

- The story of Horus, the Sun God of ancient Egypt tells of a boy born on the 25th of December to the virgin Goddess Isis, the only begotten son of the God Osiris and as such, was part god, part human. His birth was announced by angels and witnessed by shepherds. Jesus was born of a virgin, the only begotten son of God, on the 25th of December. His birth was also announced by angels and witnessed by shepherds.

- The star Sirius announced Horus' birth. A star in the east announced Jesus' birth.

- Horus had a foster father Seb, which Greek /Roman translates to Jo-Seb (Joseph) who was of royal descent. Jesus' foster father was Joseph who was also of royal descent (blood line of David).

- Both Horus and Jesus have nothing written of them between the ages of 12 and 30 and are baptized at age 30 in a river by an assigned baptizer who was later beheaded.

- Horus spent time in the desert and mountains to be tempted by his archrival Set (who was a precursor for the Hebrew Satan). Jesus was taken from the desert in Palestine up a high mountain to be tempted by his archrival Satan. Both resisted temptation.

- The grown man Horus had 12 followers or disciples, who traveled with him as he preached his philosophy, performed miracles, performed exorcisms, was considered a prophet, healed the sick, restored the sight of the blind, and stilled the water with his power so as to walk on it. Jesus had 12 disciples who travelled with him as he preached; he performed miracles, exorcisms, healed the sick, restored sight to the blind and stilled stormy waters so as to walk on them.

- Horus raised Osiris, his dead father, from the grave. Jesus raised Lazarus, his close friend, from the grave.

- Horus' most famous address was the "Sermon on the Mount". Jesus' most famous address was the "Sermon on the Mount".
- Horus was betrayed by a friend, Typhon and he was consequently crucified beside two thieves, then burred in a tomb and after three days was resurrected. Horus' resurrection was announced by two women. Jesus was betrayed by his disciple Judas, was crucified next to two thieves, was buried in a tomb and was resurrected after three days. Jesus' resurrection was also announced by two women.
- Horus promised to return to Earth to reign for 1000 years. Jesus made the same promise to return to Earth to reign for 1000 years.

It doesn't stop there though:

- Mithras of Persia was born of a virgin on the 25th of December, was crucified, placed in a tomb and resurrected after three days.
- Krishna of India was born of a virgin, the lady Devanki. A star in the east announced his coming. He performed miracles with several disciples, died and was resurrected.
- Dionysus of Greece was also born of a Virgin on December 25th, was a traveling prophet who performed miracles and turned water into wine.
- Attis of Phrygia was also born of a virgin Nana on the 25th of December, was crucified, buried in a tomb and was resurrected after three days.
- Even the silly story of King Herrod wanting to kill the baby Jesus that led to the new family escaping to Egypt is a direct echo of the tale of Moses' at the beginning of Exodus.

Do you get the point? The story of Jesus is as original as my mother's 'famous homemade pizza', with 100% fresh ingredients... it even comes in a handy box with 'Domino's Pizza' written on the front... how convenient! My point is simple, Javier, the story of Jesus is fabricated fantasy, and as such, every little act of horror that has been enacted upon humanity in His name, is the direct result of this exaggeration. Thus, there is great danger in exaggeration, so stop deluding yourself.

By the Grace of God

You say that everything depends on God's grace and the correspondence (prayer) of Christ's followers over successive generations, but this is completely unsupported by a little thing called 'evidence'. Whilst I do realize that 'evidence' is not something that Christians either heed or need, but seriously, there have only been a handful of *objective* studies performed on the efficacy of prayer and every single one has found prayer to have NO EFFECT... EVER!

In fact, one of the most recent studies on prayer and its effect on human physiology (specifically neurology) showed that prayer and meditation activate the part of the brain most commonly associated with imagination and creativity. So when you consider that God has failed to act on ANY-BLOODY-THING since the he left Holy Spirit stains on Mary Lewinski's loincloth, it doesn't make a compelling case for the efficacy of prayer, does it?

Regardless of who or how hard ANYONE was praying to Him, literally nothing happens. It simply doesn't make a very compelling case that anything, ever has or ever will depend on God's grace, or the prayer of His loyal, albeit deluded, peons!

Indoctrination and Evangelism

Like hundreds of millions of children around the world, I was indoctrinated into the Catholic theology. As such, I know just how effective you and your bastard sheep are at evangelizing your horribly malevolent doctrine. Based on this, it sickens me to tears that you take joy in 'proclaiming the Gospel to the ends of the earth'.

The indoctrination of children is a most abhorrent practice, but I do realize that without poisoning these young children to believe in your definitive testament of continual historical inaccuracy, Catholicism would not survive to poison the next generation. I wasn't sexually abused, though many, many were and most likely still are today.

While I appreciate that none of the priests of the churches I attended abused any of my brothers or I, I will never forgive having the notion that 'faith will always trump evidence' being drilled into my skull from an early age. I will never forgive the church for teaching bigotry against homosexuals, against the friends who I grew up with – good, intelligent men who just happened to be gay. I will never forgive Catholicism for preaching misinformation about sex, condoms, and 'the evil and empty promises of science'.

Contrary to your beliefs, Javier, today there is an urgent need to dismantle and discredit 'Christ's doctrine' and most especially in the areas that you mention; government, science and research and those people working in the field of public opinion. Personally, there are few things that disgust me more than when a supposedly secular government is called to make a conscience vote on a pioneer medical advancement that will improve the lives of countless millions around the world, and instead of being impartial and ethical, they side with their chosen theocracy's view on the issue.

We've seen this happen countless times over the past several years, whenever the contentious issue of embryonic stem cell research (the most cost effective and abundant method for harvesting healthy stem cells for research) is raised, or euthanasia or abortion. The issue goes to Congress for discussion and vote, and is shot down on the grounds that the religious assertion that 'life starts at conception', instead of 'when the fetus develops a nervous system' (months later). Because of this, stem cell researchers have to harvest stem cells from living donors, which is excruciatingly painful to the donor, horribly expensive (because drugs are required to liberate the stem cells into peripheral blood) and ultimately produce very few stem cells. Not to mention the fact that the embryos used in embryonic stem cell research are the leftovers from IVF treatments, which would be otherwise incinerated.

We're talking about life saving and quality of life improving medical research that will eventually cure Multiple Sclerosis, Muscular Dystrophy, Motor Neuron Disease (which Stephen Hawking suffers from), Alzheimer's disease, Diabetes, spinal cord injury, Parkinson's disease, Heart and Cardiovascular Disease, Lung Diseases, Arthritis, genetic defects, and a plethora of others. Even with this impressive list of 'promises' behind it, Christian stupidity prevailed, forcing this medical research to take a back seat in many countries.

In the USA, now that the previous injunction (which was specifically related to "ending life for the purposes of research) enacted by Bush has been partially repealed (awaiting hearing), researchers will spend the next 10+ years literally playing catch-up. Over the eight years where Bush reigned supreme, the USA lost all of their experts and technological supremacy to countries that were pioneering in this lifesaving research.

So, you'll have to excuse my antipathy towards your message of ignorance, misinformation and stupidity being spread, or 'evangelized', further across the globe.

The Time For Tolerance Is Over

In a perfect world, religious people would be tolerated, but because their views are based on fantastic delusions of grandeur that have remained unchanged for two whole millennia; their views should never be revered, supported or used to oppose any form of actual progress in human civilization. Whenever a religious person spoke, one would listen intently, then raise one's eyebrows, give a coy smile and pat them on the head, saying, "you hang in there sunshine, you're frigging special"... even though they're *totally* not.

You say that all of us, and by that I assume you are referring to humanity as a whole, need to listen to God's voice and follow it, but again I find your terminology, "God's voice" oxymoronic. After all, if God had a voice, faith would not be required for religiosity, there would only be one religion and human suffering would not exist. What you are actually referring to as 'God's voice' is the voice of the Catholic Church, which is better described as the Voice of Malicious Ignorance.

On a side note, I deeply loved that month or so between the death of the old Pope and the election of the new one. For a few weeks, there is not a single person alive claiming infallibility that is not otherwise locked up in a mental health facility.

Invariably, Christianity has spent the better part of the last 2,000 years giving a voice to God and ensuring that everyone in the Western world heard it. Put more eloquently, the Vatican has held the ears and the brains of Western humanity in captivity for almost two millennia and has done nothing positive with it.

It has not furthered humanity's understanding of the universe, it has not cured disease or prevented war or famine – it has done the exact opposite. Christianity has the view that everything that needed to be learned was learned 2,000 years ago and systematically fought (and in many cases, won) against any attempt to truly advance humanity.

Every opportunity for advancement has been looked upon with contempt and ridicule, you've kept some of the greatest minds imprisoned or just killed them. You've (the Catholic church – guilt by association) told your flock to burn books; you've murdered and committed genocide all in the name of keeping things under your rule. Worse, you've made people feel guilty for EVERYTHING, especially those things that are completely natural, like sex and sexuality, yet covered up the abomination of the sexual abuse of children by clergy.

In my mind, the only thing that separates the Catholic Church from a monarchy is that often a monarchy is actually concerned for the welfare of the people under its charge. Your stupid, petty little theocracy is only concerned with *your own place* in the lives of the people under your charge. Javier, all that Catholicism has done for the last 2,000 years is hold humanity back from progressing beyond you. This dogmatic view of the universe is no longer relevant; every scrap of knowledge acquired by us today teaches that blind faith in ANYTHING is ridiculous. And that's the good news!

God, A Great Big Dick-tator

God has no voice, if it/he/she did, it sure as hell wouldn't need you or your flamboyant little club of perverts and pedophiles with pointy hats, now would it? The Catholic Church has a voice, so does Christianity in America (just ask Pat Robertson or Rick Warren), but God is without voice. If God were not carried in the brainwashed minds of individuals like you, Javier, he would never have been carried out of Egypt or Jerusalem. For without the legs, mouths and gullibility of the faithful believers, he has no legs to stand on.

If God does exist, and he wants to be followed, revered and worshiped, let him/her/it come down and give us reason to believe. Random and arbitrary threats of eternal punishment only make him appear as a fickle, malicious and utterly reprehensible dictator and the threat of violence is no reason to respect or revere someone. Bullies should be ignored and they should never be followed.

No matter how loving you portray God to be, the Bible shows us the polar opposite. Your god *is* vile.

With the above in mind, it sickens me to think that yet another generation will be taught of the Church's faith based ideals of anti-abortion, anti-euthanasia, anti-homosexuality, anti-contraception, and anti so many other stupid arbitrary laws that you've enacted upon humanity.

There is a Catholic run hospital close to where I live that is about to have a major government funded expansion and will become one of the largest children's hospitals in the state. The problem I have with this is the mandate that the Catholic Church has which enforces the 'right to life in all its phases'. This means that children born severely premature are 'saved' but most live very short lives in excruciating pain. By no means am I saying that these 'preemies' don't have a right to life, but the life that they have is in most cases, no life at all.

One only needs to visit their local old fogies' home to see the effects of the Catholic Church on a person's right to dignity. My own Grandfather, once a brilliant, vibrant and spirited man, was felled by dementia and Alzheimer's and had to sit in a nursing home which prolonged his life for two years which he specified he never wanted to live. Euthanasia is banned in Australia, as it is in most countries in the western world, and it is mainly because when this topic is discussed in parliament, the supposedly secular ethical discussion becomes a deeply religious debate. People, like my Grandfather, should have the right to die with dignity.

Religious Schooling

You say that people should have the right to choose an educational format for one's child that corresponds to each one's spiritual and moral ideals, but where is the child's choice in this? When does the child get to have a say in whether they be taught evolution or creation; taught of the cultural significance of all religions or the subjective, convoluted and twisted truth as seen from

147

one the perspective of a your vindictive and judgmental religious eyes? Teaching a child that one particular viewpoint is the only valid viewpoint (i.e. I'm right, it is impossible that I am wrong, and you are wrong), is completely contrary to intellectual development and invariably is the basis for every religious war or battle that has ever occurred.

When you teach a child that the Catholic view of the world is the only one with credence, then they will grow up believing that Satan and demons and sin lurks around every corner, when it only exists in the convoluted teachings of that silly little fairy tale dogma of yours! There is a very good reason why state school children from the non-redneck states of America (California, Massachusetts, New York, and Illinois) aren't taught mandatory creationism; it is because it has been refuted. Utterly refuted! Religious belief is belief in spite of contrary evidence, belief in spite of reason and logic; teaching this to children is like teaching a two year old how to take the safety off the AK-47 you gave her for X-Mas.

You say, "we should consider carefully, how we have helped souls to get closer to God: how much prayer, how much sacrifice, how many hours of well-done work we have offered, how many conversations we have had with friends, relatives, colleagues, acquaintances". How do you help someone get 'closer' to something that by all rights, by all evidence, does not exist? To be clear, I am not one of those anti-theists/atheists who claim that science is the answer to everything; Gods have existed in the hearts, minds and fears of humans since the crucible of civilization, but we have no proof of any one god's existence over any other. No, if you look objectively at

148

the last 2,000 years, i.e. since Christianity, Islam and Judaism became the only way to have a personal relationship with God, we have countless situations where an all-powerful, all-loving God could have stepped in to circumvent. God didn't, ipso facto, objective proof that God doesn't exist. Clear as mud?

Jesus Idolatry

So you claim that Jesus Christ should be revered as a model?

> *[Jesus replied], "And why do you break the command of God for the sake of your tradition? For God said, 'Honor your father and mother' and 'Anyone who curses his father or mother must be put to death.' But you say that if a man says to his father or mother, 'Whatever help you might otherwise have received from me is a gift devoted to God,' he is not to 'honor his father' with it. Thus you nullify the word of God for the sake of your tradition. You hypocrites! Isaiah was right when he prophesied about you: 'These people honor me with their lips, but their hearts are far from me. They worship me in vain; their teachings are but rules taught by men.'" (Matthew 15:3-9 NIV)*

Nice one Jesus, I'll totally go and kill my children for disrespecting me now... after all, if Jesus said it, it must be righteous, right?

> *Now Jesus' mother and brothers came to see him, but they were not able to get near him because of the crowd. Someone told him, "Your mother and brothers are standing outside, wanting to see you." He replied, "My mother and brothers are those who hear God's word and put it into practice." (Luke 8:19-21)*

Did Jesus just disrespect his Mom? Oh no he didn't! Oh yes, he did!

So while Jesus' belief was that a disrespectful child should be killed, apparently the laws given to Moses by Jesus' Daddy didn't apply to Jesus.

> *[Jesus said] "Woe to you, teachers of the law and Pharisees, you hypocrites! You build tombs for the prophets and decorate the graves of the righteous. And you say, 'If we had lived in the days of our forefathers, we would not have taken part with them in shedding the blood of the prophets.' So you testify against yourselves that you are the descendants of those who murdered the prophets. Fill up, then, the measure of the sin of your forefathers!*
>
> *"You snakes! You brood of vipers! How will you escape being condemned to hell? Therefore I am sending you prophets and wise men and teachers. Some of them you will kill and crucify; others you will flog in your synagogues and pursue from town to town. And so upon you will come all the righteous blood that has been shed on earth, from the blood of righteous Abel to the blood of Zechariah son of Berekiah, whom you murdered between the temple and the altar. I tell you the truth, all this will come upon this generation. (Matthew 23:29-36)*

Jesus on a stick - he's one feisty guy once you get some wine into him, isn't he! Jesus was a total rock star, prima donnas Rabbi! A few little technicalities in Jesus' little ranty diatribe though, none of his prophecies came to fruition, not within the generation he prophesied, not ever... then again, Jesus was never very good with the follow-through on his prophecies... rapture anyone?

What about *Matthew 15:22-26*, where Jesus calls a Canaanite woman a dog when she asks Jesus to cure her daughter of a demonic possession? That's not cool, Jesus, that is not cool at all. And how about this little doozie:

[Jesus said] "Therefore I tell you, do not worry about your life, what you will eat or drink; or about your body, what you will wear. Is not life more important than food, and the body more important than clothes? Look at the birds of the air; they do not sow or reap or store away in barns, and yet your heavenly Father feeds them. Are you not much more valuable than they? Who of you by worrying can add a single hour to his life?

"And why do you worry about clothes? See how the lilies of the field grow. They do not labor or spin. Yet I tell you that not even Solomon in all his splendor was dressed like one of these. If that is how God clothes the grass of the field, which is here today and tomorrow is thrown into the fire, will he not much more clothe you, O you of little faith? So do not worry, saying, 'What shall we eat?' or 'What shall we drink?' or 'What shall we wear?' For the pagans run after all these things, and your heavenly Father knows that you need them. But seek first his kingdom and his righteousness, and all these things will be given to you as well. Therefore do not worry about tomorrow, for tomorrow will worry about itself. Each day has enough trouble of its own."
(Matthew 6:31-34)

Is this why all Americans are fat? They're just munching away like there's no tomorrow, waiting for Jesus to descend on a cloud and smack the BigMac out of their hands... Good advice Jesus! Jesus also mentioned a certain distain for other religions in the above passage.

"[Jesus said] So in everything, do to others what you would have them do to you, for this sums up the Law and the Prophet." (Matthew 7:12)

Finally, some good stuff from Jesus. Problem is though that Both Buddha and Socrates said the same exact bloody sentence 500 years earlier, Moses said it as he was on his way across the desert in *Leviticus 19:18* as well. The difference between Buddha, Socrates, Moses and Jesus however is that Jesus' little rehashing of the Golden Rule came with a scary addendum: be good or burn in Hell-fire for all eternity. If I were gullible and deluded enough to be a religious person again/still, I reckon I might choose a religion with a little less violence or fewer threats of eternal torture… or at least one with a more wholesome, good and empirically supported deity.

Women; What Women?

Now, moving onto your anti-feminist sentiments, Javier. Women, well at least in my opinion, are like a fine wine; they cost lots of money, stain the carpets when you punch them and have a 50:50 chance of being really tasty or horribly expensive vinegar. All jokes aside, compadre, you're opinion on women is a little out dated. Our society (Western) has always been a patriarchal one and as a consequence, the sacred feminine has, for thousands of years, taken a subservient back seat. In Catholicism, for whatever reason, you won't even let women become priests. The side of our species that *is* compassionate, that *is* thoughtful and loving is apparently incapable of interpreting the word of God (i.e. the word of the Vatican). I think you're just afraid of women intruding on your little boys club. You are kidding yourself if you think for one archaic second, that the role of the male is any more or less significant than that of the female in any heterosexual relationship.

It is high time for men around the globe to take a more active role in their household so that everything is split 50:50 and the fairer sex don't have to feel the stupid guilt that institutions like the Catholic Church have been drumming into their head for centuries. Stop imposing these archaic anachronistic, guilt ridden decrees that women don't deserve to be happy in whatever they do.

Feminism may well have begun with the sexual revolution, but it was empowerment to finally take control of one's own life that drove it to its height. Finally, women are free to do what they want, whenever they want, to whoever they want, whilst wearing whichever red or black latex ensemble they wish, and all you can do is relate it back to a fear of having more children?

Seriously, Javier, sex is, as you say, 'anthropologically and socially irrelevant, something purely phys-iological'... not that you'd know anything about that, would you now? I'd be very interested to know how you, a giant celibate cross-dresser (not that there's anything wrong with that), could ever claim to know anything about sex. Keep your Jesus off my penis!

Love is just another form of deep caring and attachment, a desire to protect and be protected, which is echoed throughout the mammalian and even avian species. Hell, you only need to look at a colony of bacteria under a microscope to see just how closely knit our ancestors from 4 odd billion years ago are.

Sex is bloody brilliant too! But to claim that it is anything more than physical is simply arrogant. Sex is like everything in life, the more you do it, the better you get, the more people you practice with, the more experiences and encounters you have, the better and more enjoyable it is. I'd love to discuss this more with you, Javier, but it feels kind of irrelevant considering the stupidity of celibacy. To believe you were created by God, yet deny the physical nature of the human animal, which is ultimately, sad.

I dare say that the reason the Catholic Church has had such an overwhelming number of cases of sexual abuse on children is because of this fact, a consequence of forcing people to deny a part of what makes them human. It stands to reason that they would lose some of their humanity (i.e. the part of your brain that says "this child trusts me to care and nurture, not rape and torture") in the process!

Also, being the son, husband and father of highly intelligent, aggressive and beautiful women, I feel compelled to point out that there is nothing at all wrong with a woman that knows what she wants. Personally, I find a most admirable quality in anyone, but most especially in women/girls. The repression has gone on long enough!

I do agree that the latent inferiority complex that exists in the female psyche needs to be eradicated, but this inferiority is something still so prevalent in Catholicism today. Hell, you only need to look at the front of a church to see the male priest and the male altar boys. It's as though you're saying that women are equal to men in every way... except this way, and this, and that and this and that.

"All humans are equal... it's just that some are more equal than others."

How Anachronistic Are You?

With regards to pornography, I'd be a liar if I said I didn't partake. Hell, women have to make money. Also, going back to your point on the anthropological and purely physiological aspects of humanity; I have hormones and desires. Pornography is useful, it's entertaining and it fulfills a purpose for most men and most women, so you'd have to conclude that it is both harmless and bloody awesome! How much seed have you spilled?

With respect to abortion, I deeply respect a woman's right to choose.

It is curious though that Catholics, all Christians in fact, are so staunchly and idealistically opposed to abortion, but literally couldn't care less about what life the child would have once born. Having an abortion leaves an emotional scar with the woman that will stay with them for the entirety of their life.

Having said that, an abortion, in many cases, wouldn't be necessary if you'd get off your fat Catholic asses to promote the wide spread use of condoms and other birth control! Seriously, you pope-wannabe, if you were to make a positive change in the world of today, and tell Catholics all over the world that while you may not agree with anonymous, promiscuous sex with hot strangers, if you're going to do it (which they always have and always will) put a condom on!

Your objection to divorce is hilarious though. Instead of setting each other free of a relationship that, despite all hard work, does not work, you condemn them to Hell on Earth? Wouldn't it just be better to allow both adults to find their next 'true love'? To me though, Catholic marriage just seems like little more than ownership with some occasional missionary position sex thrown in. Without mutual love, attraction, interaction and seriously hot sex, marriage ceases being a union and instead becomes a prison.

If there were such a thing as a God, Javier, I would think that that it would be far more concerned with its creations happiness, over the depth of their demented and depraved servitude. You Catholics get so bogged down in your hilariously flamboyant rituals and costumes, that you've totally missed the point of life - to experience *EVERYTHING!*

Catholicism has it all wrong; where you could be telling people to go out and have fun, to experience life and all of its splendors, instead, you prefer your stupid and archaic traditions, your silly rituals and your blood and gore filled effigies to sadomasochism (which you refer to as "church"). If I were Jesus, I would be so pissed at you right now!

Yours in Blood/Flesh Sacrifice for Redemption, Javier,

Jake Farr-Wharton

How Can You Have Morality Without God?

William Lane Craig is an American Evangelical Christian apologist, theologian, and analytic philosopher known for his work in the philosophy of religion, historical Jesus studies, and the philosophy of time. He is one of the most visible contemporary proponents of natural theology, often participating in debates on the existence of God.

The following is an excerpt of his comments in a debate with Kai Nielson at the University of Western Ontario.

Friedrich Nietzsche, the great atheist of the last century who proclaimed the death of God, understood this all too well. "The end of Christianity," wrote Nietzsche, "means the advent of nihilism." Only the man who is able to live beyond good and evil will acquire mastery in the coming age of nihilism, which stands already at the door. I think the specter of Friedrich Nietzsche must haunt every atheist. For if there is no God, then why wouldn't nihilism be true?

Notice carefully what we're asking. The question is *not*, "Must we believe in God to live moral lives?" I would say, "No." *Nor* is the question, "Can we recognize objective moral values without believing in God?" I would say we could. *Nor* is the question, "Can we formulate a coherent system of ethics without reference to God?" That is perfectly possible.

Rather, the question is, "Do objective moral values exist if God does not exist?" I don't see any reason to think that, in the absence of God, human beings would have objective moral value. After all, if there is no God, what is so special about human beings? They're just accidental by-products of nature, which have evolved relatively recently on in infinitesimal speck of dust, lost somewhere in the heart of a hostile and mindless universe, and are doomed to perish individually and collectively in a relatively short time. And if push came to shove, I think Professor Nielsen would agree with this. Although he says that he holds to objective moral values, he's using those terms in an idiosyncratic way.

To say that objective moral values exist is to assert that statements of moral value like "Rape is wrong" are true independent of whether anyone believes them or not. But Professor Nielsen declines to discuss the truth of moral statements. And so he, like Ruse and J. L. Mackie, cannot seem to affirm the objective value of human beings.

But the fact is that objective values do exist, and we all know it. There is no more reason to deny the objective reality of moral values than there is to deny the objective reality of the physical world. In particular, it is evident that evil exists. Some things are really wrong! And thus, paradoxically, evil actually serves to establish the existence of God.

For if objective values cannot exist without God, and objective values do exist–as is evident from the reality of evil–, then it follows inescapably that God exists. Thus, although evil in one sense calls into question God's existence, in a more fundamental sense it demonstrates God's existence, since evil could not exist without God.

Dear William,

You have certainly been a busy lad in your own personal crusade to debate atheists wherever you can find them. You've taken on some big stars in the world of philosophy and theology, including Messers, Walter Sinnott Armstrong, and Ray Bradley amongst others. In each of these debates, you held your own with your all too predictable convoluted philosophical arguments blended with a little voodoo science. But then you ventured where angels dare tread, throwing down the gauntlet to Christopher Hitchens, author of *God is Not Great*. He, of course, gave you a good ole fashioned horse whipping that would have made any Madam Lash blush in any of the most extreme S&M clubs anywhere in the world... not that I would know anything about that... I frigging swear!

To put it even more frankly, Hitchens was all over you like a fat kid on a Big Mac. His riding you like Miss Daisy - porno version of Driving Miss Daisy - has me all revved up to give you a little spanky-spanky too. So drop your drawers William and get ready for something real special... I won't be gentle, but only because you've been such a naughty little boy.

Objectivity, We Must Have Objectivity

In reviewing the comments from your debate, the essence of your argument can be abbreviated into three headlines:

- If there are objective moral values then God exists.
- There are objective morals.
- Therefore, God exists.

Lurking behind your argument is the theist belief that we cannot be good without God. Naturally, I, as a non-believer, believe that morality has nothing to do with a sky-god command giver.

If your species loathing assertions were true, then explain to me why is it that we CAN think of objective sources for moral order that DO NOT require the existence of an order driven God? Whilst we are YET to have a conclusive scientific study on understanding human morality it does seem obvious that love, sharing, and cooperation are more conducive to human pleasure than hate.

Are the moral laws self-evident? Of course they are, silly. Are morals subjective to culture? Of course they are, dummy. Now you use the crime of rape as an example, as will I. In short:

1. Rape is morally wrong! FACT. Even if some group residing somewhere on the planet thinks otherwise, they are wrong.

2. Rape is morally wrong because it causes harm to another person. Inflicting physical and emotional pain. These harms are not justified by any benefit to anyone else. This is an objective observation.

3. In the Bible, God commands us not to rape. *"If a man happens to meet a virgin who is not pledged to be married and he rapes her and they are discovered, he shall pay the girl's father fifty shekels of silver. He must marry the girl, for he has violated her. He can never divorce her as long as he lives."* (Deut 22:28). But why should we obey God's commands? Invariably, you will answer that God has good reasons for his commands and that we should obey. Thus God commands us not to rape because it harms another person, the victim. But, then, it is the harm that makes rape immoral not the command. Therefore, rape would be just as harmful without God, and just as immoral without God.

Conclusion: Rape is immoral and God is superfluous.

If we think of morality in terms of harm, then rape is objectively immoral. It's the harm on another individual that makes it so.

The Trolley Dilemma

Let us now reference this against the sky God of Abraham who commands us that 'Thou shall not rape', notwithstanding the fact that what God really means in context is that 'thou shall not rape a fellow Israelite, but knock yourself out with your pagan worshipping neighbors'. God makes this command because it causes harm and suffering on our fellow man. Therefore, it is the harm that makes rape immoral, rather than the command. Let me illustrate this with another example, as well known that it is in philosophy circles, the Trolley Dilemma:

First Scenario: A trolley, or train for you non-Americans, is hurtling down the rail track at top speed. Unknown to the trolley captain, up ahead are five workers performing maintenance to the track, who will undoubtedly be killed by the trolley within moments. However, you, the unfortunate bystander, are standing near a lever that once pulled will divert the trolley onto another track, thus saving the lives of the five workers. Problem – there on the other track is a single worker doing his job who will be surely killed by your actions.

The question is: Is it is acceptable to pull the lever to kill the one person instead of the five?

Second Scenario: Similar to the first there is trolley heading down the track towards to the five workers who will undoubtedly be killed, you again are the unfortunate bystander but in this instance you are standing on a bridge that spans over the track. Standing next to you is an obese man. Due to his size, you are sure that by pushing him off onto the track will ensure the trolley comes to an halt prior to reaching the five workers, thus you have killed one man to save five.

The question is: Is it morally acceptable to push the bystander off the bridge?

William, I know you may view this as a juvenile hypothesis and I am sure you have heard similar versions of the same situation, but the aforementioned scenario strikes a devastating blow to your argument. How? Well, assuming you respond in the same manner as the overwhelmingly vast majority does, you will have chosen to, without much hesitation, to spare the lives of five men by sacrificing the life of one. Fair enough! However, your response to the second scenario is probably a little more problematic for you. You may or may not have elected to push the obese men off the bridge, but it is likely that, after making your decision, you figured out a way to rationalize your decision.

As I mentioned, the trolley dilemma is one that has been philosophized exhaustively, and while intellectual enthusiasts have hypothesized numerous solutions to the second scenario what makes the dilemma interesting is that the bystander is faced with the identical scenario – kill one person to save five. The question we must ask ourselves, William, is why, then, do a majority of people hesitate on the second scenario but not on the first?

Psychologists have reasoned that the answer has to do with two conflicting parts of our brain. One part of our noggin is dealing with the rational, utilitarian decision; whereas, another more primitive part of our brain is dealing with our hardwired emotional response.

Returning to the respective scenarios once more; in the first, all that's required is to pull a lever. The workers seem like equal players in the game, so losing one has to be better than losing five, and moreover there is little or no emotional engagement for the bystander. However, the second scenario requires the unfortunate bystander to take a physical action against the innocent obese man i.e. pushing him off the bridge, which ultimately will ensure his death. This triggers a basic, emotional response within our grey matter; a reaction that screams you should not inflict harm on another person. Therefore, we can reason that the hesitation that people experience in examining the second scenario is that the human brain is at war with itself, between its rational and emotional data warehouses.

What if we make the scenario even more complex by assuming that the obese man on the footbridge is a friend or relative of yours? Bearing in mind that you jumping is not an option in this hypothetical. What do you do? Would you push your own child from the bridge to save the five workers? What if the person was an enemy, would you push him then? My point being that the answers to these questions can't be found in the Bible, they are not objective they are subjective, and based on emotions.

There have been litanies of studies that use this scenario to examine the brain and moral decision-making. One such study published in the journal *Nature* in 2007 found that people who had suffered damage to the emotional centre of the brain make vastly different moral judgments than people with healthy brains. In an article citing this study as featured in the *New York Times*:

> *"I think it's very convincing now that there are at least two systems working when we make moral judgments," said Joshua Greene, a psychologist at Harvard. "There's an emotional system that depends*

on this specific part of the brain, and another system that performs more utilitarian cost-benefit analyses which in these people is clearly intact."

Tying this study of the human mind back to your argument in which you assert that without God, morality is arbitrary rather than objective, surely this recently acquired scientific understanding has the 'wake the hell up' alarm bells ringing?

How can morality be objective when we can demonstrate that our moral decisions are governed by subjective emotional responses? The decision to push the fat man off the bridge or not is a decision, if faced by you or me, is made in the moment, prior to any detached and unbiased thought process can take place. Therefore this is not a dilemma that can be reconciled with a religious code of ethics or behavior, because the dilemma innately creates conflict within our brains at a biological level.

Before you return fire with the counter claim that the trolley dilemma is an unrealistic hypothetical, we can apply this to a real life setting. Let's take Sumatra, Indonesia, for an example, following the tsunami that decimated the coastal regions of that island. Consider for a moment the situation presented in any of the hundreds of hospitals in the hours and days after the tidal wave struck. Tens, more probably, hundreds of thousands of injured and dying people converging on the hospitals for urgent medical attention. The moral dilemma that first caregivers are faced with, are:

- Which patients to be treated as a priority?

- Which patients warrant the allocation of the limited hospital resources?

The answers to these questions are not objective moral decisions that lend themselves to simple solutions that could be echoed as one-liners from the Bible; they are complex decisions whose outcomes will be determined in the machinations of many doctor's minds. A conflict between the emotional and rational components of our brain.

We can see clearly that the dilemmas confronted in such a scenario also highlight the biological and evolutionary nature of morality. The key point I am making here is that our moral judgments are primarily subjective, emotionally driven decision; logical rationalizations of these decisions invariably follow rather than precede them.

This is where you, predictably so, disingenuously attempt to create a false dilemma by suggesting that without sky-god authority, we have only our cultural whims to discern between right and wrong. Without God, everything is possible, isn't that what you say? However, such a self-loathing worldview overlooks the overwhelming importance of moral judgments in our evolutionary history, and our human experience.

We Are Animals
We are members of a species that are innately interdependent on one another for all aspects of our mental and physical well-being. The principle of 'you scratch my back, and I will scratch yours' is evident all around us.

Our species is not alone in sharing these traits better known as the social contract. Even the chimpanzees have figured this out without the need for a sky-ape to watch over them. Why can't you accept the fact that chimps are intrinsically programmed for altruistic behavior such as taking care of their young and elderly; performing roles in social teams; and are able to compete for social promotion for what zoologists label the principle of social service.

How do chimps manage this without a God inspired objective standard? If you cannot answer that then maybe you are still in awe of Kirk Cameron's peeling of a banana as he explains how well shaped the banana fits to a human hand as proof of God's creation. By his logic it means that the shape of our penis is better suited to jerking off rather than coitus and therefore the perpetuation of our species.

Moreover, paleontological evidence shows that in our current form, i.e. homo sapiens, homo erectus, Australopithecus (and many others), we have occupied the Earth from anywhere 50,000 and 250,000 years. If God, according to the Bible, gave man his moral instructions in the form of the Ten Commandments only 4,000 years ago, how then did we make it 46,000 to 246,000 years as a species without committing self-annihilation?

Specifically, how did the Assyrians, the Ancient Greeks, the Ancient Egyptians, Mesopotamians, Babylonians, Native Americans, Indigenous Australians, Romans, and so, so many more, survive without your biblical morality? The answer is that they survived just fine. In fact, they survived so well that many of them lived in peace and solidarity right up until the time that White people invaded and brought their own stupid religion. Take for example the Indigenous Australians; they were nomadic, they lived off the land, and they lived in mostly relative peace for about 50,000 years before the British came and conquered. 50,000 years is a long time to live without sky-god morality and still survive.

To underscore this with direct biblical reference, how the hell did the Israelites manage to peacefully coexist with one another as they wandered the never-ending sand hills during their mythical forty-year desert jamboree? How did Moses and his flock not wipe themselves out through rape, murder, violence, and theft as they traveled together for four decades on the way to Mt Sinai to be delivered God's moral code? You would think that after forty-years of the Israelites complaining in the back seat of Moses' car, "Are we there yet?" that Moses would have driven the damn car off the Mt Sinai cliff.

Up to the point when God spoke to the Israelites at the fictitious Mt Sinai, there were no celestially ordained laws preventing rape, murder, adultery, homosexuality, etc – and despite the absence of the moral guidance from a celestial supervisor they managed to survive. Not just merely scrape through by the skin of their taints either, they survived fit and ready to begin their genocidal conquests over the land of milk and honey; their Promised Land. Therefore, we can only conclude from this bullshit biblical myth that laws against murder, rape, and theft were self evident, and no one in the sky was required make the Israelites play nice with each other in the world's biggest sandbox. Unless of course, you're suggesting that committing such atrocities in the name of a sky-pixie inherently makes them moral... in which case, I'll be robbing a bank in the name of God tomorrow!

Richard Dawkins, in his book *The God Delusion*, makes the point that our morals evolve with the times, as a moral zeitgeist. He uses the poignant example that it was only a generation or two ago, when no moral obligation to allow women to vote existed, mainly because they were thought of as the lesser sex. In some countries the breastier sex are still not permitted to do so. Whereas, if any man made the assertion that women should not have the right to vote at any dinner party today, he would be tarred and feathered, then used in CSI Miami – where Horatio Red-Head would say, "looks like... he was... too much of a chicken... to stay alive."

Another example is the treatment of Blacks and Jews. Go back a hundred or even sixty years and it was not accepted as immoral to refer to either race as 'inferior to whites'. Even Thomas Huxley, a social progressive by the standards of his time, wrote:

"No rational man, cognizant of the facts, believes that the average negro is the equal, still less the superior, of the white man."

No one batted an eye-lid when Huxley made this assertion, as it was at time, 1871, an acceptably morally founded statement. Imagine if any man of any prominence said anything remotely like this today; they'd be dragged behind the General Lee tied by a Confederate flag from Alabama to Kentucky.

You see, using the Bible as your guide for morality is problematic because it doesn't allow for the zeitgeist provision or progression. The Bible is a static document. God only wrote one book with no addendum or as Lewis Black wrote:

"Even if the Bible is a dead-on accurate transcription of God's words, it's rather shocking that God only had two books in him, the Old and the New Testament. I've actually written two books and I am sure God would have written more than me. Two books? That was all he had to say to us? You think he would have put at least a pamphlet in response to the Holocaust. And if not, a pamphlet, a couple of well placed fire-balls, for crying out loud. This is the Supreme Being we're talking about, who whacks Sodom and Gomorrah and turns Lot's wife to salt and Hitler doesn't get so much as a twisted ankle? It seems a little suspicious to me."

Henceforth, we are left to determine what is morally sound based on a book that demands you:

- *That upon discovering one of your wives is not a virgin on your wedding night you are to drag her by the hair to her father's house and stone her to death on his doorstep. (Deuteronomy 22:20)*

- *That a rape victim must marry her attacker. (Deut 22:28-29)*

- *Your children should be executed for exploring other religious beliefs. (Deut 13:6-10)*

- *That you may sell your daughter into sexual slavery (also Deut 22:28-29)*

- *That you may use a male slave's wife and children as bargaining chips to extort the male slave into staying on after his seven (7) year term has lapsed. (Exodus 21:2-6)*

- *That it is preferable to offer your daughters to be gang-raped by a pack of salivating drunken perverts rather than surrender a male guest that you had only met five minutes earlier. (Genesis 19:8)*

The Ten Arbitrary-mandments

Alright so what about the first Ten of the six hundred and thirteen commandments found in the first five books of the Old Testament; surely these Ten can form the basis for morality you ask? In a word, NO!

Don't forget, the Ten Commandments are claimed to be the most profound laws regarding morality because they are directly ordained by the Creator of the universe. These are the 'laws' that most of the ignorant (Christian) world believe to have formed the basis of, among others, the US Constitution and the Laws and Justice Systems of every country in the West. We also mustn't forget that most of white, Christian America believe that the Ten Commandments were what the Founding Fathers were making love to as they wove their magic to found the USA!

If this is right then it is fair to expect these 'Ten' to be inspirationally enlightening. But the truth is they are far from it. In fact Christopher Hitchens refers to the first half of the Decalogue, as nothing more than *"maniacal throat clearing."*

"Oi, you down there, it's God here. I'm the one and only. Don't even think about sampling that Buddhist gong music crap or I will kill you. Don't even think about spending the Sabbath in other means other than kissing my holy ass. And don't place me second to any other gods or I'll smite the living shit out of you!"

Thus the first four commandments have nothing do with morality whatsoever, as they merely decree how and by what means we should get down on our knees for Him (innuendo intended).

The only commandments that refer to any kind of morality are the 'Don't steal, kill, lie, commit adultery and to a lesser extent, 'be good to your parents'. The last one, 'thou shall not covet' i.e. want shit, is an Orwellian thought crime – notwithstanding that the economy of every country is literally centered on coveting thy neighbors' crap enough to want to work hard enough to earn the money to buy it! This is the best code of ethics for moral conduct the most intellectually profound being can come up with? Are you serious?

Now, let us compare God's best effort to muse on morality against that of a simple, human made effort that posted on a website (*www.ebonmusings.org*) by a blogger:

1. Do not do to others what you would not want them do to you;

2. In all things, strive to cause no harm;

3. Treat your fellow human beings, your fellow living things, and the world in general with love, honesty, faithfulness and respect;

4. Do not overlook evil or shrink from administering justice, but always be ready to forgive wrongdoing freely admitted and honestly regretted;

5. Live life with a sense of joy and wonder;

6. Always seek to be learning something new;

7. Test all things; always check your ideas against facts, and be ready to discard even a cherished belief if it does not conform to them;

8. Never seek to censor or cut yourself off from dissent; always respect the right of others to disagree with you;

9. Form independent opinions on the basis of your own reason and experience; do not allow yourself to be led blindly by others;

10. Question everything.

If a lone blogger can devise a far superior top ten for promoting human solidarity, equality, justice and ultimately, morality – then why do you impose a need for God? Surely this must prove to you that as a species we have outgrown the angry alpha pixie patriarch in the sky.

Infinite Punishment for Finite 'Crime'

Now before you go scrambling for the New Testament as your crutch for whimpering away from the barbarism of the Hebrew Bible, Jesus - *with his porcelain white skin, luscious auburn locks, who just oozes meek and mild* - is the one responsible, along with John the Baptist, for introducing us to the concept of eternal torture. A truly wicked and despicable doctrine, that Jesus is not only comfortable with but loved reminding his followers that that is what awaits those that don't kiss his sandals 24/7.

Ask yourself a simple moral question: How moral is it, how just is it, to sentence a finite sin with an infinite punishment. "Oh you screwed your neighbor's wife one time, and now you will burn every day from sun up to sun set. Tomorrow, and the day after for infinity."

There's an old joke that highlights the flaw in having a sky Master arbitrarily decide for us what is moral and what is not. The story has it that Moses ascends to the top of Mt Sinai to receive the Ten Commandments. He spends his forty days perched atop of the mountain that does not exist, before making his way to the Israelites who are having a gangbang at the foot of a golden calf. Moses summons his chosen people's attention and shouts, "I have spoken to God. He has given me ten new commandments. I have good news and I have some bad news. The good news is that the number of commandments amounts to only ten. The bad news is adultery is one of them."

The point is that according to what is known as the Divine Command Theory, as illustrated in the above joke, nothing is right or wrong unless God makes it so. Whatever God says is final. So if God had decreed that adultery was permissible, then adultery would be permissible. You believe Jesus is Lord, and then you read the text and study the various contextual problems, then attempt to reason them so they do not trouble your faith.

Incapable of Altruism

An interesting and horrifying study on religion and morality was conducted by US professor George Tamarin, who lived in Israel for many years. His study included the written replies of 1066 high school students to two questions posed to them based on the siege of Jericho as described in all its genocidal glory in the Book of Joshua. The students were asked two (2) questions:

1. Do you think Joshua and the Israelites acted rightly or not? Explain why you think as you do.
2. Suppose that the Israeli Army conquers an Arab village in battle. Do you think it would be good or bad to act towards the inhabitants as did Joshua towards the people of Jericho (and Makkedah)?

To the first question 95% of responses were in the same vein as the actual response below:

> *"The objective of the wars was the conquest of the country for the Israelites. Therefore, the Israelites acted well in conquering the cities and killing the inhabitants. It is undesirable to have a foreign enclave in Israel: The people of the different religion could have influenced the Israelis…"*

Even more chilling, the fact that Thirty per cent of the answers to the second question were categorically in favor of wiping out the inhabitants of a captured Arab village. Here comes the kicker! On a similar sample, but with a sample of 1006 different school children, kids were given the Book of Joshua to read but the names and places were changed. Instead of Israel, the story was set in China. Instead of Joshua, it was General Ling Wang. Instead of Jericho it was Mongolia.

The children were asked the same two questions: THE RESULT - ONLY 7% said General Ling Wang's actions were justifiable. Need we say more?

What is especially ironic about this is the fact that atheists are so often accused by conservative Christians of not being able to offer any reasons for being good and instead merely following the arbitrary whims of society, culture, or rulers. It's theists, or at least theists who subscribe to the divine command theory of morality, i.e. conservative Christians, who are ultimately following arbitrary whims. In the end, they themselves are unable to offer any good reasons for doing so — just the prudential "reason" of having to avoid Hell.

The avoidance of Hell is at the very foundation of every religious person's decisions or actions and it is inherently selfish. Literally, anyone capable of critical thought could assert that having such a belief makes them, incapable of any altruistic action.

So why is this an inferior form of morality?

First, there is no real moral merit in following an order - anyone can follow an order while not all orders should be followed.

Second, the ability to follow an order is more characteristic of robots and serfs, not free ethical individuals. If a person is to be lauded for their behavior, it should be because they choose the right path, not because they simply followed instructions correctly.

Finally, a morality such as this can be the most arbitrary that exists. Decisions are completely separated from their consequences for others and the impact upon one's personality. Orders are followed simply because they are given - not because they reduce suffering, not because they increase happiness, and not because they are in any way virtuous.

Ultimately, if morality was tied to God then we would see some sort of social data to confirm this, but in fact we find the opposite. The correlation between increased religiosity and social dysfunction is overwhelming. When social dysfunction is measured in terms of crime rates; teen pregnancy; illiteracy; gender inequality; per capita income; and infant mortality the bottom ranked countries in the developed world are unanimously religious, whereas the nations at the top of the heap include democratic and secular nations such as Norway, Australia, Canada, Netherlands, Denmark, Sweden, and Belgium.

It is no longer acceptable to murder your new wife for not being a virgin; it is no longer acceptable to rape or sell your daughter into sexual slavery; it is no longer acceptable to enslave another human. No one in the civilized world still uses the Bible as his or her moral compass, so why is it still revered? Religion may have guided our morality through the dark ages (and that is a point I refuse to concede) but what followed that mark of time was the period of the enlightenment, and from that point on religion had begun its exit from relevancy.

> *"The person who is certain, and who claims divine warrant for his certainty, belongs now to the infancy of our species. It may be a long farewell, but it has begun and, like all farewells, should not be protracted."*
> *(Christopher Hitchens)*

If indeed the Bible has anything to teach us of morality, it is how simple tribes people attempted to document a social contract.

Beyond this... well, I suppose you could recycle it... appropriate use of resources is a very important lesson to learn! I hear it also makes good toilet and cigarette paper... though I don't suggest using it in that order.

Yours in objective morality,

Jake Farr-Wharton

TO REV. BILL MCGINNIS

The Religion of Atheism

Dear Reader, the following is an article from Rev. Bill McGinnis, an Internet Christian minister, writer, publisher and Christian Podcaster. He is Director of *LoveAllPeople.org*, and all of its related websites including: *InternetChurchOfChrist.org, CivicAmerican.com, CommitteeForTheGoldenRule.org and AmericanDemocrat.net.*

Here is his view of Atheism as a Religion:
http://patriot.net/~bmcgin/atheismisareligion.html

A person's religion is the sum total of his beliefs about God and the supernatural. Christianity, Judaism, and Islam are the three largest "monotheistic" religions, with belief one God, the same God, Creator Of The Universe.

Some religions are "polytheistic," with belief in many gods, each with different functions. Atheism is the religion whose belief about God is that there is no God.

Some Atheists, for their own political reasons, assert that Atheism is not a religion but instead is the total absence of religion. This allows them to spread their Atheistic beliefs freely in societies which insist on "separation of church and state."

But this is like saying that "black," (which physicists define as the total absence of color) is not a color. A few years ago, the car I drove was a big, old Chevrolet, whose color was black. In common practice throughout the world, "black" is understood to be a color, despite the technical definition of the physicists. Likewise, "Atheism" is a religion, despite any technical definitions to the contrary.

If black is a color, then Atheism is a religion. A United States Federal Court of Appeals has also ruled that Atheism is, indeed, a religion, under U.S. law (July, 2007 - Illinois). If Atheism is a religion, then it must be subject to the same legal restrictions imposed by governments on all other religions. In particular, in the United States, the teaching of Atheism must be prohibited wherever the teaching of Christianity is prohibited.

But where is Atheism being taught? Atheism is being taught, by default, in all places where other religions cannot be taught, particularly in the public schools.

When the State mandates that the Theory of Evolution be taught as fact, that is establishing the religion of Atheism, because the Theory of Evolution asserts that all life forms are created not by God, but by pre-existing natural processes. This is pure Atheism! If we are not created by God, then there might as well be no God, for all the difference He makes.

The mere fact that many scientists are Atheists does not entitle them to establish Atheism as our State Religion!

When the State prohibits free discussion of God in the classroom, that is establishing the religion of Atheism. Wherever the State permits Atheistic ideas to be spread but prohibits Theistic ideas, that is establishing the religion of Atheism.

Therefore I urge you to understand clearly in your mind that Atheism is a religion, just as Christianity, Judaism, and Islam are religions. And any restrictions placed on Christianity, Judaism, or Islam must also be placed on Atheism. Atheism must not be allowed to slip through its little loophole any longer, by pretending it is not a religion.

Blessings to you in the name of the One God, Creator of the Universe. Blessings to you. May God help us all.

Dear Bill,

What you suggest is unequivocal blasphemy against the non-God of Atheism. Your punishment - as documented in the Atheist non-doctrine, *The Origin of Species* by Charles Darwin - is a deep tissue massage from no less than fifty tanned beauties of whichever sex you choose, who, in turn, will later bang your tiny little brains out.

Sounds pretty attractive, doesn't it? Well, those of us in the Atheist religion aim to please; after all, we're better and more intelligent than the rest of the world in every single way. Why not de-convert to atheism and enjoy the many, many benefits, including, but most certainly not limited to:

- being smarter
- being stronger
- being sexier
- being healthier
- being a realist
- being a rationalist
- being concerned with others well being for no other reason than 'that all deserve to be well'
- focusing on living for today rather than for your afterlife
- enjoying discussions in biology, physics and philosophy without an arrogant belief that your answer is inherently correct
- enjoying monogamous or promiscuous heterosexual sex without the indoctrinated requirement for procreation
- enjoying homosexual intercourse without fear of eternal torture after death
- being able to look at a fossil as an ancient species instead of a long running joke that God is playing on scientists
- altruism

Enough fun, Bill?

Definitions

As a logical kind of guy, I can understand your point, but I have somewhat of a problem with it. Your suggestion that "Atheism is the religion whose belief about God is that there is no God" is kind of a nonsensical non sequitur. You have just told the world that atheist belief is a lack of belief and, as such, should be considered a religion. This is like saying that all non-smokers should be considered smokers because they consider smoking as vile, or that vegans should be considered meat eaters because their view is that eating the flesh of animals is wrong. As I said, it just doesn't make sense.

The assertion that atheism isn't a religion isn't just one of those 'personal beliefs' that atheists hold, the word 'atheism' has a rather compelling etymology: from Greek *a-* 'without' + *theos* 'god'. So where a 'theist' has God, an atheist does not.

So now that we have presented something for your logical brain to contemplate, can you still seriously suggest that a lack of belief equates to belief?

The Laws of Nature Were The Gods of The Past

Religion, in its most broad definition, is belief in spite of reason, or belief in spite of evidence. One has faith that one's God both exists and cares despite the complete lack of evidence to support either belief…. Or the complete lack of evidence to support any form of supernatural forces or being. Atheism clearly does not fit into this tidy little box because the reason most atheists do not hold belief in gods is simply because of a lack of reason or evidence to suggest that such things exist. An atheist's assertion is completely within the known and understood and established patterns of the universe.

These understood and established patterns of the universe are known and referred to as the Laws of Nature. You see, while the theories governing the Laws of Nature are intangible, they are observable. Scientific Method is a process whereby theorem is continually tested, continually challenged and scrutinized for efficacy and accuracy to further our understanding of our universe and ourselves. As such belief in the Laws of Nature is not necessary.

On the other hand, you have religion. Religion asserts that humanity has an all-loving creator that is able to circumvent the laws of nature. Unfortunately for religion, all of the phenomena attributed to God/s, things like creation, natural disaster, morality, social structure and bananas are observable in nature and thus do not need to be attributed to a supernatural overlord.

The fact that we have verifiable proof that everything in nature has made an evolutionary journey to arrive in its current state completely invalidates the notion of biblical Genesis and by extension, creationism. With further extrapolation, this also invalidates the claim that the Bible is the 'inerrant and infallible word of God'.

With that said, Gods were always the 'go to' thing that the ancient civilizations used to explain unexplainable - but ultimately totally natural - phenomena. Considering there was no knowledge of understanding of plate tectonics in ancient times, when the earth shook, it meant that you'd pissed off one god or another. Following logical progression, this meant that you needed to slaughter something to appease it... after all, nothing says, "please don't kill me" by killing something. When no quakes or less severe aftershocks followed, the tribe would be satisfied that the gods had been appeased and continue on their merry way until the next time it happened.

Likewise, the ancients feared the ocean and assigned particular gods to them. So when flooding or tidal waves occurred, one could easily assume that the 'gods were angry'. "It was Tony over there, he pissed in the lake. Go kill his children to appease the gods"… As such, when humanity was ready to hollow out a log and set sail, certain ceremonies were necessary to appease the gods prior to casting off. From where do you think that prayer originated? Prayer is ritual!

Welcome to Religion

The ancient polytheists were not stupid, they were as human as you or I, they simply lacked the tools and abilities to discover their origins, and as such, their creativity, imagination and uncontrollable fear got the better of them and they created gods. Fear, especially towards death, is an incredibly powerful motivator. Unfortunately for us, humanity did not learn or comprehend that nothing can be done to appease nature, and instead of preparing for the worst, we ended up blindly praying for the best. Mind you, I'll bet more than one smart young man convinced more than one receptive young female that by having wild sex, the Gods would be pleased. Hmm, I wonder whether that still works…

Monotheism is no different. The ancestors of the Jews created the first monotheistic religion with the idea of a personal/benign god. Instead of having a god that one had to appease in order to survive, servitude to their god meant that their enemies would be vanquished by the circumvention of natural laws. Better yet, where polytheism had priests and shaman who could only interpret natural phenomena and ascribe some message from the gods, monotheism had a line of prophets who could directly speak with the single god who was responsible for *everything*.

The god of the ancient Hebrews was a vile, duplicitous and abhorrent little bugger. The first book of the Bible begins with God saying how happy he was with his creations... and then a few chapters later he is smiting the human race with a global flood as punitive damages for enjoying themselves too much. Men, women, children and all but two of every species of animal, bird and insect were killed at the hands of this homicidal and infanticide maniac who the Christians, Jews and Muslims of today worship with great and vehemence, fervor and conviction.

Enter the Purportedly Magic Jew

The dictations from God to Moses and his fellow 'prophets' were kept as law and lore for many centuries until the little heretic bastard, Jesus was alleged to have come along to change the Jews understanding of God, the universe and everything. I say 'alleged' for an extremely important reason, beyond the New Testament of the Bible, there is no evidence to suggest that he ever existed. As such, Bill I will refer to Jesus henceforth as the 'purportedly magic Jew'.

It seems preposterous to a rational mind that someone such as the aforementioned Purportedly Magic Jew, i.e. one who healed the sick, cast out demons, circumvented the laws of nature to turn water into wine and multiply quantities of food for his followers, would now be better documented in history. Unfortunately, the first mention of Purportedly Magic Jew was from the Apostle Paul, who wrote of Purportedly Magic Jew as being almost wholly ethereal and even he didn't write until anywhere from 25 to 100 years after Purportedly Magic Jew was dead. As there were indeed historians both alive at the time that Purportedly Magic Jew was reputed to have lived and who documented much within the areas where Purportedly Magic Jew was reputed to have lived, it most assuredly makes the rational, thinking and intelligent mind question the existence of Purportedly Magic Jew.

Christianity specifically remains the most observed religion in the world. But in order to believe that the Son of God, who was also God, descended from Heaven to purge sin from humanity at death whilst remembering that there is no verifiable evidence to support such a theory, takes a huge leap of faith. It requires one to completely bypass both logic and reason; two human characteristics that any proponent of God would ironically attribute back to God.

Again, this goes back to my earlier assertion that religion can be summed up as belief in spite of reason and belief in spite of all contrary evidence. There is no reasonable way to prove the existence of God or Purportedly Magic Jew beyond the historically inaccurate ramblings of the Bible. As such, Christianity, Judaism and Islam (all religion, really) require a significant leap of faith in order to bridge the gap between reality, and the supernatural overlords that their doctrines support.

What is Atheism?

Atheism, on the other hand, requires no 'leap of faith' whatsoever, for it is, as I suggested earlier, a complete lack/absence of belief. Religion requires belief, atheism is the antithesis or the absence and has no doctrine or rhetoric which one must adhere to, in order to label oneself as an atheist. Atheism is superior to religion in every way; especially in penis size... it's way bigger.

As such, referring to atheism as 'not being religious', is not, as you suggest, politically motivated; it is not a belief system; it lacks a doctrine; it does not have followers; and it does not require any leaps of faith... of a Purportedly Magic Jew. Consider that a new born child has no understanding of religious belief, holds no religious convictions and prior to their indoctrination into their parent's religious tradition has no understanding of their parents respective Gods. A newly born child cannot believe in god, because belief in god is not innate it is learned, or more specifically, taught. All newborn children are thus atheist. They are without God. And religion is, therefore, socially inherited.

Where and what are these atheistic beliefs which you purport that we atheists hold? Also, I think that you will find that the Founding Fathers of America were the ones who promoted the secular separation of Church and State, Christianity is the religious group attempting to, and heretofore is succeeding, in changing this.

The Theory of Atheism

I find it somewhat laughable that you associate the 'Theory of Evolution' with atheism. Evolution does not presume to prove or disprove the notion of God or the supernatural. It is the model to explain how all earthly flora and fauna have progressed to its current state. Of course, understanding the fact that humanity is the result of an infinite number of completely natural processes, which can indeed lead someone to the perfectly acceptable conclusion of atheism. But it is, by no means, a given.

The theorem supporting biological evolution are constantly being revised and improved, providing humanity with an ever expanding, and yet ever-clearer, understanding of our own biology and, as Charles Darwin put it, the origin *of our species*. Biblical Genesis, on the other hand, with the exception of being translated from language to language over time, has never been altered, expanded on and simply does not stand up to peer review. Well, unless the peer review is performed by a mixture of knuckle draggers, mouth breathers and the fine little intelligence terrorists at Kansas's Westboro Baptist Church.

While evolution does completely refute biblical genesis, it certainly does not refute God or the notion of gods. As such, the very notion that evolution is an atheistic propaganda ultimately shows your complete lack of understanding of both biological evolution and atheism. Intelligent scientists and science lovers who also happen to be religious find no trouble reconciling their religious belief with evolution.

Frank Collins, one of the chief scientists on the Human Genome Mapping project, is both a Christian and a believer in evolution. This man was able to reconcile his belief in God with evolution and found no conflict with his belief. If you are saying that evolution is an atheistic belief, then you are saying that this man is not Christian.

As I have often said, Billy-boy, it seems to me that detractors of evolution, those much like yourself, seem to have missed some critical step in the evolutionary process. After all, it has been argued for some time now that the great Charles Darwin, the architect of the theory of evolution, had some belief in God, for at least some of his life.

Teach The Controversy

Biological evolution - whist to some extent evolving its self over time - is fact, and has most certainly stood the test of time. As such, evolution should not only be taught in schools, but it should be taught as the *only* theory explaining our origin. Why? Because teaching evolution and intelligent design or creationism side by side as equally viable theorem is literally suggesting teaching fact and fiction side by side, while equally passing both off as fact.

So, if we decide to teach the 'controversy' with respect to biological evolution, should we teach the other 'controversies'?

- When astronomy is taught, should we also teach astrology? "Mrs. Smith, I can see the moon through the telescope, but how do I get my moon into this house of Sagittarius... am I doing this right?"

- When chemistry is taught, should we also teach alchemy? "Mr. Gregson, I was able to get the explosive reaction when I mixed the potassium permanganate and glycerin, but I can't seem to turn this lead into gold... am I doing this right?"

- When biology is taught, should we also teach of the creatures of ancient Greek mythology? "Miss Thomas, I can't seem to find a satyr or centaur on the fossil record... am I doing this right?"

Do you get the point, Bill? It is completely unreasonable to enforce your dogmatic notions of biblical genesis on people who are unable to discern between fact and bullshit! And before I go any further, I do feel obliged to make the point that your doctrine, i.e. the book you've based your belief system on, is unequivocal centaur crap!

Just because you and your foolish creationist friends lack the cognitive fortitude to understand evolution, does not mean that it should be discounted from the classroom. Give children the opportunity to succeed where you have failed and we may all end up living in a more productive society.

Your website suggests that you are a proponent of literal biblical interpretation, and being that you have already asserted where children are taught 'the atheistic belief of evolution' they should also be taught creation, I thought I should do you a solid and just relate to you the funny stuff that you believe kids should be taught. As a 'biblical literalist' Christian, I'm sure you're aware that you believe:

- in Dragons: Deuteronomy 32:33, Job 30:29, Psalm 74:13, Isaiah 27:1, Jeremiah 9:11, Micah 1:8

- in Satyr, a creature of Greek mythology: Isaiah 13:21, Isaiah 34:34

- in a sea monster known as a Leviathan: Job 3:8, Job 41, Psalm 74:14, Psalm 104:24-26, Isaiah 27:1

- in Unicorns: Numbers 23:22, Numbers 24:8, Deuteronomy 33:17, Job 39:9-10, Psalm 22:21, Psalm 29:6, Psalm 92:10, Isaiah 34:7

- in Cockatrice, a serpent hatched from a rooster's egg that can kill with a glance: Jeremiah 8:17, Isaiah 11:8, Isaiah 59:5, and Isaiah 14: 29

- the earth is flat: Daniel 4:11, Job 38:13, Isaiah 11:12, Jeremiah 16:19, Revelation 7:1

- the earth doesn't rotate around the sun: 1 Chronicles 16:30, Psalm 93:1, Psalm 96:10, Psalm 104:5, Isaiah 45:18.

- in giants: Genesis 6:4

- in witches and sorcery: Exodus 22:18, Deuteronomy 18:9-14, 2 Chronicles 33:6, Galatians 5:19-21

- that the stars, suns from hundreds of thousands of light-years away, can fall to the earth: Revelations 6:12-14

Can you seriously tell me that you want that stuff taught to children at school? Young, impressionable minds open to influence and suggestion, especially from those selling their 'information' with conviction, as you do. What are you going to say when the smart kid in the class asks "where is the evidence?" or "why isn't there a unicorn in the fossil record?" Are you going to teach the children to laugh at the smart kid for questioning religious doctrine as they did in my class, in my Christian school and in schools around the world? It certainly shut me up quickly!

Sure, as a Christian, you cherry pick the bits and pieces of the Bible that you believe in whilst banishing the rest to absurdity. Ultimately, if you believe in a 'literalist interpretation' as your website and articles suggest, then you are - like many of the religious nut-bags before you - completely ignoring contrary logic and evidence so as to connect the pretty imaginary dots between natural phenomena and your imaginary supernatural God.

While atheists may indeed find common ground in their mutual passion for truth, reason and science, there is no set doctrine that one must adhere to in order to be an atheist.

That said, we atheists are pretty quick to jump on the moral and intellectual superiority bandwagon when amongst fundamentalists of the 'other side'. The problem isn't atheists not fully understanding the theorem that makes up evolution, the 'big-bang' or string theory. I'm certainly not precluding that potential issue, but the actual problem is when atheists, in trying to prove a point or shut down a creationist argument, make an audacious claim that is not evidence based. I've seen it happen a dozen or so times (and probably done it myself), and it's not pretty!

I am fortunate enough to have Orthodox Jewish, Christian theologians and practicing Muslims as friends and have had plenty of scorching and utterly thought provoking discussions about the nature of gods, spirituality, rationality and general philosophy. We have a great time over beer, wine, water, and pork chops, and while we all respect/tolerate each other's beliefs, or lack thereof in my case, we pull no punches in challenging each other. We are educated, well-spoken and very passionate people with a wealth of worldly experience and have a great time discussing religion. It can be done Bill, you just need to lose the silly little

Christian Creationist prejudice and penchant for assumed supremacy.

My religious friends have been pushed by their respective religious institutions, as I can tell that you were, to propagate the belief that atheism is a religion and that, as such, it should be put under the same restrictions as the other religions. Luckily for them, however, I was able to set them straight and show them that the only commonality between any two atheists is their lack of belief in gods.

Sure, there are plenty of atheists who believe in evolution, but I tell you in all seriousness, Billy-boy, the only thing stopping you from 'believing' in evolution is simply not understanding it.

You see, the problem most religious detractors of evolution have with the 'theory' is they were told by some religious authority, who claimed to have read Darwin's *Origin of Species*, that the 'theory' is just a 'theory'. They then claim that so called 'evolutionists' think there were monkeys and, then, *poof* there were humans. Anyone who understands evolution knows that this is not the claim or the case. Evolution just requires you to think in terms of tens and hundreds of thousands, or millions, or billions of years. This is the complete opposite to how we, as finite beings with a one hundred year maximum expiry date, are hardwired to think.

Move beyond your theology, move beyond your propaganda and simplistic notions of a personal God who creates and destroys as he sees fit. Go back to university and learn biology, physics and mathematics and teach these worthwhile and important subjects to your children and the children in your congregation.

Open your mind to the facts that are accepted by the best and brightest that humanity has to offer and give the next generation a chance to supersede you and your personal understanding of the universe; move beyond the fiction and the bullshit.

Most importantly, remember; if atheists are correct, then blasphemy is a victimless crime!

Hedonistically yours,

Jake Farr-Wharton

TO DR. PAUL NYQUIST

The Inerrant Word of God

Dr. Paul Nyquist was unanimously appointed as the next president of the Moody Bible Institute by the Moody Board of Trustees and began his tenure as Moody's ninth president on June 1, 2009. He served as president and CEO of Avant Ministries from 2001 to 2009. Before joining Avant, he served as senior pastor at First Federated Church in Des Moines, Iowa from 1996 to 2001, and Evangelical Bible Church in Omaha, Nebraska from 1983 to 1996. He graduated from the University of Nebraska at Lincoln with a bachelor of science in Architectural Studies in 1976. He received a Th.M. in 1981 and a Ph.D. in Systematic Theology in 1984 from Dallas Theological Seminary.

We believe that the Bible is God's word. The doctrinal statement of Moody Bible Institute affirms, "The Bible, including both the Old and New Testaments, is a divine revelation, the original autographs of which were verbally inspired by the Holy Spirit."

Revelation is God's self-disclosure. It is God making Himself known to men.

God has revealed himself in a limited way in creation.

But the Bible is a form of special revelation. The Bible is "special" revelation in the sense that it goes beyond what may be known about God through nature.

It is divine in origin, since in the Bible God makes known things which otherwise could never be known. The Bible is unique because it is God's revelation recorded in human language.

According to II Timothy 3:16–17 the words of Scripture are "God breathed" or inspired. This implies that God is the source or origin of what is recorded in Scripture. God, through the Holy Spirit, used human authors to write what He revealed in the Bible. They were not mere copyists or transcribers. The Holy Spirit guided and controlled the writers of Scripture, who used their own vocabularies and styles but wrote only what the Holy Spirit intended.

This is true only of the original manuscripts, not the copies or translations. Although the original manuscripts have been lost to us, God has preserved the biblical text to a remarkable degree. The Bible is verbally inspired. This means that the words of the Bible, not just the ideas, were inspired. What is more, this is true of not just some, but all the words of the Bible. As a result, the Bible is free from error in what it says. Moody Bible Institute believes strongly in the factual, verbal, historical inerrancy of the Bible. That is, the Bible, in its original documents, is free from error in what is says about geography, history and science as well as in what it says about God. Its authority extends to all matters about which the Bible speaks.

It is the supreme source of our knowledge of God and of the salvation provided through His Son, the Lord Jesus Christ.

It is our indispensable resource for daily living.

Even though the Bible is God's revelation, it must still be interpreted. Interpretation has to do with our reception and understanding of that which God revealed and recorded.

Revelation is a divine act. Interpretation is a human responsibility. Divine inspiration guarantees the truthfulness of God's word but not the accuracy of our interpretation. The Bible is infallible in all it affirms to be true and therefore absolutely reliable. We, however, may be fallible in our interpretation of the Bible.

Dear Paul,

As President of the Moody Bible Institute I am writing to you in order to air my concerns that you are lying en masse. Either that, or you are more delusional than the guy who invented the 'Catholic Condom'. Why the harsh indictment, you wonder? Well, you are the President of America's leading fundamentalist whack job school, passing off Bachelorettes more readily and easy than Chris Harrison, the host of ABC's find a husband reality show. Moreover, you are allowing your students to call themselves graduates when you have failed to teach them critical thinking or genuine textual criticism. Graduates of Moody leave with the belief that the Bible is the inerrant word of God, as it says so in your school's declaration above. To be inerrant means to be void of error. Just one single mistake voids the Bible's claim of inerrancy, and in turn makes what you believe to be a divinely inspired book a very human book.

So let's examine how human your Holy Book truly is, and once we have completed this exercise you can go ahead and post a retraction on your website. Deal? Cool let's proceed.

What Do We Know?

You write, "the Bible God makes known things which otherwise could never be known." What are you smoking dude? The forward-looking scientific or factual claims made are put forward by what can only be that of first century man. Instead of treating people who have a fever with an exorcism, wouldn't you expect this to be the moment Jesus, the Son of God, should have introduced us to Germ Theory of Disease, rather than have to wait another 1800 years for some croissant eating French dude to figure it out?

We are talking about the Son of the Creator, and in his entire thirty-three years on Earth, what revelation or discovery did Jesus reveal to us? He said something about a camel and a needle; the rich suck ass; much about sheep being lost; sons that splurge on hookers and card games instead of working hard; mustard seeds are the smallest seeds of all (but they're not); and forget about being concerned about your health, saving money, child care, or investment.

But what about revealing hidden secrets whose disclosure would have benefited man in a tangible way? Jesus, allegedly, healed a blind man; but how about a cure for blindness? Jesus, allegedly, healed a leper; but how about a cure for leprosy? In other words, Jesus revealed things to us that only a man living in 30 AD could have told us, nothing more.

Moreover, the Bible tells us that rainbows are a symbol of His covenant with us, but it says nothing about the light refraction and spectra (i.e. the actual cause of rainbows). The Bible says the Earth is flat (but, it's not). The Bible says the sun revolves around the Earth (but, it doesn't). The Bible says the sun goes to sleep in its tabernacle at night (but it doesn't). I can go on but I think my point has been made – God revealed nothing in the Bible that humanity did not, or could not, have discovered all by its self.

The Weight of Words

In the next breath, you demonstrate your complete ignorance of textual criticism and manuscript transmission in quoting 2 Timothy, "God Breathed the words of Scripture." The Book of 2 Timothy was not written by Paul! It is a forgery, a fact , that is universally accepted as true by all reputable modern day scholars, which by correlation excludes you and your school from being a reputable institution of Biblical scholarly. Allow me to have the world's preeminent New Testament scholar, Bart Ehrman, break it down for you:

> *"Regarding the Pastoral Epistles of 1 and 2 Timothy and Titus, there is even less scholarly debate than in the cases of Colossians and Ephesians. Among critical scholars teaching in North America, the United Kingdom, and Western Europe – the leading areas of biblical research – the consensus of opinion for many years has been Paul did not write these books......There are 848 different Greek words used in these letters, of which 306 do not occur anywhere else in the letters allegedly written by Paul in the New Testament. This means that over a third of the words are not Pauline. Something like two-thirds of these non-Pauline words are words used by Christian writers of the second century." (Jesus Interrupted, page 129-130)*

You then write, "God, through the Holy Spirit, used human authors to write what He revealed in the Bible. They were not mere copyists or transcribers. The Holy Spirit guided and controlled the writers of Scripture". Problem being, we don't know who the key authors were. We have no idea who Matthew, Mark, Luke, or John were, and if those were their real names.

We don't even know their respective nationalities; presumably they were highly educated, and wealthy Greeks from a large urban centre such as Athens, or Rome. Far removed from the illiterate, peasant class, Aramaic speaking followers of Jesus. Therefore, your proclamation that the authors were not mere copyists or transcribers is a fallacious one, because we have no clue who wrote the originals, and who wrote the early copies.

Where Are All The Originals

You do get one thing correct; you are right in saying the original manuscripts are lost, but then you tag behind that statement, a whopper of fallacy, "God has preserved the biblical text to a remarkable degree." Firstly, how do you know what God's word was, when we simply no longer have his original words? There are some pretty darn big assumptions floating about in your mushy mind. You're making huge presumptions that run in complete contrast to what we do know; and what we know is this:

1. We no longer have any of the originals. We only have copies of the copies.
2. We have 5,700 copies or manuscripts of the Greek New Testament.
3. Those 5,700 copies contain a total - are you ready for this - of at least 400,000 textual variances i.e. changes/alterations.

Therefore, the next question you need to ask yourself is this: with so many variants, why were these changes made by scribes?

Well, there were innocent accidental changes i.e. slips of the pen, slips of the eye, incorrect spacing which changed the translation of words. However you claim that, "God through the Holy Spirit guided and controlled the scribes". If that were at all true, why then, did God allow more than 400,000 errors, changes, and variations? Is God really *that* sloppy?

If God did, as you infer, co-author the Bible then his effort is as sloppy and careless as his was in creating the Earth! You know what I mean; most of the Earth is either too hot or too cold to sustain human life; 99% of all living creatures which have ever walked the face of the planet are now extinct; and so on, and so on. The fact that God couldn't ensure that we preserved his original words, and the fact we have more variations than we have words in the Bible should concern you.

You've Got To Have Faith

Paul, it's one thing to have a faith and practice it in the privacy of your own home, synagogue, or church but when you start promoting this bullshit with the specific purpose of attracting new students, then that's where you and I have problems. These books of the Bible did not fall from the sky; the copies we have are the product of the penmanship of human hands. In fact, they are often from the hands of barely literate scribes - particularly until the fourth century before the profession of transcribing documents became a meal ticket.

Now here's my next question, are you aware of how we have come to inherit the copies that we have today? No? Well, let me wrap it up for you:

The Bible had its genesis in the same manner that all books from antiquity were created; word of mouth. Remember there was no Twitter 2,000 years ago, nor was there print media. As a matter of fact, and I'm sure this will come as a complete surprise to you; Jesus' entire life story is built on fourth, fifth, and fiftieth-hand verbal accounts by people who not only never met Jesus, but also never met the people who met the people who met Jesus.

Now I am going to write the number for the total sum of records we have of Jesus nearly one hundred years after his alleged death: 0

Alumni Are A Real Bitch

Now, I mentioned the name Bart Ehrman in a paragraph or two earlier, do you remember a former student by that name? Well, he enrolled in your school in 1973 before graduating with his three-year diploma in 1976. Ehrman then went onto Wheaton College before completing his PhD at Princeton Theological Seminary. Ehrman became an ordained a minister and spoke about God from the pulpit, but his lifelong studies of biblical texts began to gnaw at his insides much in the same manner a 2am gas station burrito does to me.

He went onto become the Chair of the religious department at the University of North Carolina and has now authored a total of twenty books on the New Testament, three of which have made it onto the New York Bestseller list. He is now the world's leading scholar on New Testament studies. This fact is amazing considering that he was ultimately unable to reconcile the aforementioned 400,000 variations within the numerous manuscripts with his faith and soon became an agnostic. Hallelujah, he's truly seen the light.

Having given Dr. Ehrman such an introduction, I will let your former student explain to you how it is that we got the copied manuscripts we have today. Take it away, Bart:

"I am a coppersmith who lives in Ephesus, in Asia Minor. A stranger comes to my town and begins to preach about the miraculous life and death of Jesus. I hear all the stories he has to tell, and decide to give up my devotion to the local pagan divinity, Athena, and become a follower of the Jewish God and Jesus his son. I then convert my wife, based on the stories that I repeat. She tells the next-door neighbor, and she converts. This neighbor tells the stories to her husband, a merchant, and he converts. He goes on a business trip to the city of Smyrna and he tells his business associate the stories. He converts, and then tell his wife, who also converts.

This woman who has now converted has heard all sorts of stories about Jesus. And from whom? One of the apostles? No, from her husband. Well, whom did he hear it from? His next door neighbor, the merchant of Ephesus. Where did he hear them? His wife. And she? My wife. And she? From me. And where did I hear it from? An eye witness? No, I heard it from the stranger who came to town.

This is how Christianity spread, year after year, decade after decade, until eventually someone wrote down the stories. What do you suppose happened to the stories over the years, as they were told and retold, not as disinterested news stories reported by eyewitnesses but as propaganda meant to convert people to faith."
(Bart Ehrman, Jesus Interrupted)

Such Accurate Propaganda

You still believe the "...the Bible, in its original documents, is free from error in what is says about geography, history and science as well as in what it says about God."

WTF? Free of geographical, historical, and scientific errors? Paul, are we really looking at the same book, or have you guys at Moody made your own? I tell you what there is, a plethora of factual errors, and here's just a tasty bite size sampler for you:

The authors of the Bible believed the earth was flat, and that at night time the sun went below the edge of the earth into his own little cubby house:

> "Their line is gone out through all the earth, and their
> words to the end of the world. In them hath he set a
> tabernacle for the sun, Which is as a bridegroom
> coming out of his chamber, and rejoiceth as a strong
> man to run a race. His going forth is from the end of
> the heaven, and his circuit unto the ends of it: and there
> is nothing hid from the heat thereof." (Psalm 19:4-6)

You see, Paul, the sun goes into its house, its little tabernacle for a nap.

The writers again describe the earth not as a sphere but as a flat immovable surface with four corners anchored down, as per the following passages:

- *I Chronicles 16:30: "He has fixed the earth firm, immovable."*
- *Psalm 93:1: "Thou hast fixed the earth immovable and firm..."*
- *Psalm 96:10: "He has fixed the earth firm, immovable..."*
- *Psalm 104:5: "Thou didst fix the earth on its foundation so that it never can be shaken."*
- *Isaiah 45:18: "...who made the earth and fashioned it, and himself fixed it fast..."*

The Bible truly is a flat-earth book, and you don't see that as a factual scientific error?

Now let's look at just one such geographical error through examining *Mark 11:1-11:*

> *As they approached Jerusalem and came to Bethphage and Bethany at the Mount of Olives, Jesus sent two of his disciples, saying to them, "Go to the village ahead of you, and just as you enter it, you will find a colt there which no one has ever ridden. Untie it and bring it here. If anyone asks you, 'Why are you doing this?' tell him, 'The lord needs it and will send it back shortly.'" They went and found a colt outside in the street, tied at a doorway. As they untied it, some people standing there asked, "What are you doing, untying the colt?" They answered that Jesus had told them to, and the people let them go.*

> *When they brought the colt to Jesus and threw their cloaks on it, he sat on it. Many people spread their cloaks on the road, while others spread branches they had out in the fields. Those who went ahead and those who followed shouted, "Hosanna! Blessed is he who comes in the name of the Lord! Blessed is the coming of the kingdom of our father David! Hosanna in the highest!" Jesus entered Jerusalem and went to the temple. He looked around at everything, but since it was already late he went out to Bethany with the twelve."*

The dilemma for you being that if we flick a few pages back in our respective Bible we read in *Mark 10:46,* that Jesus was in Jericho. However, the passage above shows Jesus and his disciples were traveling from Jericho to Jerusalem via Bethphage and then Bethany. This, however, is quite impossible and utter nonsense.

Bethany is further away from Jerusalem than Bethphage is. The Biblical theologian, D.E. Nineham, comments:

> *"The geographical details make an impression of awkwardness, especially as Bethphage and Bethany are given in reverse order to that in which travelers from Jericho would reach them...and we must therefore assume that St Mark did not know the relative positions of the two villages on the Jericho road..."*

Explanation? A great number of scholars doubt that the anonymous author of Mark was neither a Jewish individual nor a native to Palestine due to the prevalence of a number of geographical errors, mistakes and confusions the gospel attributed to him. If the author was a native of Palestine, and a Jew, then why did he appear so clueless towards the region's geography?

The answer is - drum roll - the Gospels were most likely Greek nationals who lived in an urban centre such as Rome or Athens. A number of facts support this claim:

- Jesus spoke Aramaic.
- The Gospels wrote in Greek.
- Literacy rate in the Roman Empire, at the time, is said to be less than 10%. The skill of reading and writing was reserved to those with access to money and time i.e. the ruling elite, and the bourgeois darling who, except for a few exceptions, lived in the cities.
- Jesus' disciples and followers were Aramaic speaking peasants who caught fish, herded goats, or collected taxes with strong arm tactics in the rural regions of Galilee and would have known the geography.

In tying the above four points together, we can assume the Gospel authors were Greek speaking rich bastards who lived in the larger, urban districts of the Empire. This is why geographical errors are so prevalent throughout the gospels.

99% Error Lite*

Paul, I ask you again. You still believe the Bible is free of a single error? You do? Alright, let's examine a damning historical error; that of Matthew's, 'Massacre of the Innocents' claim.

The author of Matthew writes that Herod became troubled when emissaries from the East came to Jerusalem, talking about a star and the prophecy of a new king of the Jews.

Herod asked the magi (or "wise men") to confirm the prophecy by searching out the child and then to bring back news of his whereabouts. The dignitaries agreed and departed. After discovering Jesus and presenting him with gifts, the writer of Matthew reports that they were warned by God not to return to Herod. When Herod realized the wise men would not be returning, he ordered a raid on the village of Bethlehem with the specific purpose of slaughtering all of the town's children under the age of two years.

Is there any contemporary evidence that such an event took place? No, there isn't. Not a single document from the first century attests to such an event. And while absence of evidence does not guarantee evidence of absence, this is story is regarded by historians as a fable of pure fiction. The author of Matthew, who tried desperately to tie Jesus' life to Old Testament prophecies and stories in an attempt to appeal to (and convert) a Jewish audience, took from the story of Moses for inspiration.

Eerie similarity! The Pharaoh of Egypt becomes concerned of rumors of a Hebrew deliverer or prophet, and thus He orders all male children below age of two to be slaughtered. Such a massacre would certainly have been noted by contemporary historians. Yet not even Josephus, who documented Herod's life in detail, mentioned this event.

Simply, the weight of evidence is against you. If you still believe in the Bible's inerrancy then you probably still think O.J. is innocent. Remember, one error and the book is errant. Are you so blinded by faith (ignorance) that you are unable to accept and acknowledge the most fundamentally accepted facts?

Your rhetoric flows like that of a used car salesman selling faulty automobiles. You have a faulty or flawed product but you have rehearsed the counter-objections so much so that they have become your mantra. You 'inerrantists' are a declining minority. Your particular brand of your fundamentalism is unique, and you're standing alone at the Alamo. The farewell is near, and like all farewells it shouldn't be protracted.

Belligerently Yours,

Jake Farr-Wharton

God Hates Fags

Religious broadcaster Pat Robertson said God's wrath is looming over a nation headed for economic ruin in his annual predictions for the coming year, aired on "The 700 Club." Robertson, has a tradition of ending each year in a prayer retreat and sharing what he believes God tells him during that retreat later at a chapel service for staff of the Christian Broadcasting Network and Regent University. For 2010, Robertson said, God gave him a more general warning of judgment for America's acceptance of abortion, gay marriage and secularism.

His full address can be found here:
www.abpnews.com/content/view/4690/53

"What he is telling me, and I believe is right, is that there is a cloud over this nation now," Robertson said. "There's a cloud of God's wrath over America."

"This country has enjoyed tremendous blessing," he continued. "We have been blessed like no nation on the face of the Earth, and yet we have forsaken the Lord."

"You can't have your courts turn against me," Robertson said the Lord told him. "You can't have legislation that is anti-God. You can't foster in your midst things that I call an abomination. You can't do that. And if you do, sooner or later judgment's going to come."

"God will not bless a nation where abortion is commonplace, homosexuality is institutionalized and government-sanctioned prayer and Bible reading are banned in public schools."

"Fifty million babies slaughtered," he said, in reference to abortion. "It exceeds the slaughters of antiquity."

"How can we pray for his blessing when we have that going on and when we have courts that have ruled repeatedly against him?" he asked. "We have the Bible taken from the schools. We have prayer taken from the children, and now we have perversion that God calls an abomination – we have that legitimized and given a constitutional standing by the court."

"We are engaged in a slow time of financial ruin," he said. "This country will be ultimately bankrupt. It's just a question of how soon. We're beginning that. That's one thing that I can say for certain that is happening. It's a dangerous thing. It's going to hurt America very badly. It is a problem not so much of government policy but human greed."

"I would love to say the Lord told me it's going to be peace and prosperity and it's wonderful and that God's going to bless America, he's going to bless you, he's going to bless your business, you're going to make a lot of money in the stock market and everybody's going to be happy. I can't say that."

Dear Pat,

Many years ago, in a Sunday school far, far away; a young boy of eight was being taught the 'rules of life' by his Sunday-school teacher. I'm sure that you'd be delighted to learn that the crux of her doctrine was very similar to yours, Jerry Falwell's (may he rot in Hades), and good old Fred Phelps; homosexuality is wrong; abortion is murdering babies; euthanasia is deplorable; Muslims are evil; all other sects of Christianity are wrong; and the Jews deserved the holocaust.

Can you believe that this morally repugnant drivel was taught to children? I swear on a stack of biology textbooks that this woman made us recite her little doctrine of targeted hatred word for word, every week. If we couldn't do it, we weren't allowed to do anything 'fun', like color-in those silly cartoons of Jesus on the cross and Jesus being baptized or the 'virgin' Mary participating in an orgy just prior to being raped by God. Unlike many of the other boys and girls who attended that Sunday-school, I stayed with Christianity for many more years, essentially up until my late teens when I had a wonderfully cleansing experience.

Impotent Omnipotence

"There's a cloud of God's wrath over America", so says Pat Robertson, the Prophet who profits!

Pat, if there is a cloud of God's wrath over America, then the notion that God is 'all loving' can be dismissed. If God is unable to quash the 'cloud of wrath' then God is not all-powerful. If the 'cloud of wrath' is in fact a manifestation of God's jealousy towards those who are not your particular brand of Christianity, then God is really a petty little teenage bitch, obsessed with remaining at the top of her popularity ladder.

So which one is it, Pat, is God all loving or just a whiny, bitchy teenage girl craving attention? I hear Ritalin is quite effective against that!

I've always been fascinated by the recurring tactics that religious figureheads, such as yourself, feel compelled to use in order to spread God's or Jesus' 'message'. You'll either profess God or Jesus' love, or you'll tell of the horrors that await those who do not worship them. Seriously mate; it's a broken record playing the sound of fingernails scraping on a chalkboard over and over and over and over. We've heard it all. There is no evidence to back up your pissy little claims, so move on!

God's wrath is on America, why?

You claim that it is because America has forsaken the Lord ☹.

See, I think you've got this the wrong way around; I think that the Lord has forsaken America for so damn long now that America has decided to reciprocate. We can cite a number of valid reasons why America would feel forsaken; a civil war; AIDS; spiraling foreign debt; a crippling depression; no universal healthcare (we'll see, Obama... maybe next century); widespread poverty; sky-rocketing unemployment; and so many others.

Here's, the thing; if God exists, then He has either allowed or directly caused all terrors and horrors ever experienced by believers and non-believers throughout time, all around the world. Why? If one has the power to prevent/stop harm but does *literally* nothing, then it is no different to them having caused it directly!

If *any* living person were responsible for *any* of the multiples of atrocities that God personally committed in the Old Testament (i.e. from slaughtering the first born of every non-Israelite in Egypt as per Exodus, to slaughtering entire populations of cities in every book before and after Exodus), they would be imprisoned for life at best, or placed in front of a firing squad at worst.

Consider that God, being all-powerful and all loving, could subtly manipulate the genes of babies that are born with a disease such as Down's Syndrome while they are still in the womb. Once the Down's Syndrome baby is born, most require an operation to fix an intestinal obstruction which, if not tended to, will leave the newborn in excruciating pain for the hours or days it takes to die. Even then, they will live a short life and have many medical complications associated with their genetic defect. If God is all-powerful, all good, all knowing, all loving and actually gives a shit, surely He could alter the child, whilst still in the womb, to be born healthy?

So if *He* could ensure that all babies are born healthy and yet He doesn't, then what sort of God is He? This is an easy question for atheists to answer, but how about you, Pat, what does your belief tell you?

America, the Lost Sheep

Pat, you infer that America has lost its way, well, how about God? Who decides what is moral or immoral for God? Christians have been telling us for years that we will pay for our finite sins with infinite torture and, as such, are accountable to God, but who is God accountable to? Seriously Pat, you claim to talk to God, well, let him know that I want to speak with his supervisor, right bloody NOW!

You say that America *was* 'blessed', well, when exactly was that? Don't get me wrong, Pat, I am not disputing that it may seem that *some people may* have been blessed, people like you, who have raked it in whilst spreading God's message of 'wrath-clouds'. Hell, you're almost 80 and still have a full head of hair and if one were to believe the press reports, you're able to leg press 2000 pounds, which is almost a full thousand pounds over the world record (Google "Pat Robertson leg press"). So for people like you, it certainly may well appear as though you are blessed, but what about the good Christian families living under bridges, who struggle just to make enough money to buy food or medicine or healthcare or education?

America has never been blessed, it is a country of hard working people who aspire to be better and do everything to realize their dreams (with some exceptions, obviously). I do realize however, that it is very hard to see all of the pain and anguish from a high up on your golden and white marble pedestal, high up in the clouds above!

Anti-God Legislation

You then go on to say that you can't have legislation that is 'anti-God', but this is a supremely ignorant (I refuse to believe that you're simply naïve) point of view. Whilst I've covered this topic in other letters, Pat, I'll give you a quick refresher:

- The US constitution does not mention "God" once, and the first mention of religion is: *"no religious Test shall ever be required as a Qualification to any Office or public Trust under the United States."*

- Article 6 of The Constitution and the 1st Amendment serve to separate religion from government all together.

- The words "In God We Trust" weren't printed on American coins until 1863 after a religious surge during the Civil War, the phrase wasn't added to paper money until 1957.

- The words, "One Nation Under God" were added to the pledge of allegiance in 1954 by congress. Prior to this, it read; *"I pledge allegiance to the Flag of the United States of America and to the Republic for which it stands, one nation, indivisible, with liberty and justice for all."*

- Many of the founding fathers were both publicly and proudly either deist (no organized belief, similar to agnosticism) or atheist. This included Thomas Jefferson, Benjamin Franklin, James Madison, John Adams, Thomas Paine and even George Washington.

- The original boat people who sailed to America to start afresh were ultimately seeking respite from religious imposition/persecution (i.e. they were prudes who wanted to marry their cousins).

With this in mind, Pat, one would need to go against the US Constitution and *insert* pro-God legislation before one could *replace* it with anti-God legislation. Such an act would be vehemently denounced by Glenn Beck... unless it was done by a republican. What surprises me, Pat, is that you once attempted to run for president of the United States, yet you are apparently ignorant of Her history!

An Abomination!

The things that you refer to as abomination, Pat, are bloody innumerable. Seriously though, I'm surprised that you haven't come out denouncing tampon use or the showing of affection by men "in the name of God."

For argument's sake though, let's stick with the two main things that you purport to hate; homosexuals and abortions After all, Jerry Falwell, Fred Phelps and you all publicly blamed the September 11 terror attacks on abortion and homosexuality in America.

I suppose that in a manner of speaking, you do have biblical support for your assertions:

> Do not lie with a man as one lies with a woman; that is detestable. (Leviticus 18:22 NIV)

> If a man lies with a man as one lies with a woman, both of them have done what is detestable. They must be put to death; their blood will be on their own heads. (Leviticus 20:13 NIV)

> There shall be no whore of the daughters of Israel, nor a sodomite of the sons of Israel. (Deuteronomy 23:17)

Compelling shit, right Pat? Well, compelling insofar that it may be these three lone verses have given rise to a whole generation of super-bigoted Christian douchebags, much like you. Today's Christians, especially your pals, the Evangelicals, Fundamentalists and Biblical Literalists of the bunch, use these verses for a very important and very Christian purpose; being loud and proud hate filled homophobic bigots.

Hell, every now and then, you might get together with groups of your white male buddies, get drunk on beer and schnapps and talk how much you hate this guy and that guy, but totally love that big hunk of deity, Jesus. You'll eat pizza and Butterfingers and if it's a really special occasion, you might all dress up in audacious costumes and parade around town asking for better rights. Sounds a little gay to me!

Argumentum ad Populum
Riddle me this, Pat; can you remember a time when someone great said something prolific, inspirational or captivating? Did you laugh, clap and cheer and jump on their bandwagon? Did you want to go around town to tell everyone what this inspirational person said and did and how much it changed your life? ... And then the

bomb is dropped. Think Michael Richards (Kramer from Seinfeld) racist rant (check it on youtube.com); or Biblical King Ahab who was anointed as King of Israel then started worshipping other Gods, or Pastor Ted Haggard's preaching creationism, good Christian values and hatred of gays who gets caught with a male prostitute with coke up his nose.

When those sorts of things come out of the closet, so to speak, everything that those people have done and said previously is immediately invalidated, they lose all of their credibility and their careers are all but over. Makes sense right? I mean, you wouldn't follow a general into battle after he changed his great battle speech from something like the *"we shall fight them on the beaches"* speech by Winston Churchill to *"Hopelessly devoted to you"* as sung by Olivia Newton John in Grease. Would you?

So you get it, right? Well, Pat, I don't think you do, because those Leviticus laws that denounce homosexuality are, to the rational mind, completely invalidated by the verses that precede and follow them. For example:

> *If a man lies with a man as one lies with a woman, both of them have done what is detestable. They must be put to death; their blood will be on their own heads.*
> *(Leviticus 20:13 NIV)*

Piece of cake, very straightforward, God is saying that if two dudes have sex, what they're doing is detestable and they deserve to die for it. Ok, fair enough, this isn't by any means the most graphic or violent decree given or act perpetrated by God, so it sounds as though he's being rational and even handed, the dude just doesn't like bum sex. He showed that by destroying Sodom and Gomorrah.

But then he goes and says:

> *Do not cut the hair at the sides of your head or clip off*
> *the edges of your beard. (Leviticus 19:27 NIV)*

Why, in God's name, does God give a crap about the way that I wear my hair or beard? I have a stylist God, and she told me to wear my hair like this, so bugger off! Why the hell aren't the Soldiers of The Lord - the KKK, the American Nazis, and your lot, the Fundamentalists, the Creationists and the Biblical Literalists going crazy over a distinct lack of facial and head hair? Frigging hypocrites.

Actually, I say that in jest. Obviously, I realize that shaving your beard is not on par with having sex... unless you're shaving your beard whilst having sex. So let us examine something with a similar punishment to the death to all homos verse:

> *For every one that curseth his father or his mother shall*
> *be surely put to death: he hath cursed his father or his*
> *mother; his blood shall be upon him (Leviticus 20:9 KJV)*

So there you have it, the penalty for disrespecting your parents is, in biblical terms, on the same level as bonking the man you love. So Pat, why aren't the moral crusaders for Christ not petitioning the funerals of soldiers killed in Afghanistan and Iraq with signs claiming that terrorism and war is the direct result of America's tolerance of unruly children as they do with their signs denouncing homosexuality?

For me, this lone verse completely invalidates Leviticus, if not the whole bloody doctrine. I cannot even fathom why, unless I had a son named Oedipus, I would - let alone could - ever kill my progeny! Much less for simply being a little uppity or cursing me.

Jesus on a stick, Pat! As I write this, my eldest daughter is going through that lovely hormonal change from girl to woman, so if it were my moral obligation to stone her to death every damn time that she talked back to me, told me to get lost, whispered something scathing under her breath at me, slammed the door on me, told me that I was 'too old' to understand, then I probably should have done away with her a long time ago.

Ultimately, while Leviticus may have made absolute moral and ethical sense back in ancient biblical times, it holds none today. In fact for the last 1600+ years, it has had less relevance than the pope's blatantly flamboyant attire (not that there's anything wrong with that).

So Pat, why is your moral-legion taking one quote from one paragraph of one chapter of one book of the Old Testament of the Bible and calling that 'the divine law of God' and 'that which must be followed', but not any of the multitudes of others? Why are your jizz-guzzlers of Christ not killing their own unruly children? They certainly spend a whole lot of time and energy telling gays that they're an abomination, blowing up gay nightclubs and ensuring that gay marriage stays illegal.

With that said, while the last biblical quote completely invalidated Leviticus for me, why don't we dig out a few more stupid and impractical Leviticus laws, just to make sure you get the point:

- *If a man commits adultery with another man's wife – with the wife of his neighbour – both the adulterer and the adulteress must be put to death. (Leviticus 20:10)*

- *And if a man lie with a beast, he shall surely be put to death: and ye shall slay the beast. And if a woman approach unto any beast, and lie down thereto, thou shalt kill the woman, and the beast: they shall surely be put to death; their blood shall be upon them. (Leviticus 20:15-16)*

- *And if a man shall lie with a woman having her sickness, and shall uncover her nakedness; he hath discovered her fountain, and she hath uncovered the fountain of her blood: and both of them shall be cut off from among their people. (Leviticus 20:18)*

- *A man also or woman that hath a familiar spirit, or that is a wizard, shall surely be put to death: they shall stone them with stones: their blood shall be upon them. (Leviticus 20:27)*

- *"Bring out of the camp the one who cursed, and let all who heard him lay their hands on his head, and let all the congregation stone him. And speak to the people of Israel, saying, Whoever curses his God shall bear his sin. Whoever blasphemes the name of the LORD shall surely be put to death. All the congregation shall stone him. The sojourner as well as the native, when he blasphemes the Name, shall be put to death. (Leviticus 24:14-16)*

- *"Say to Aaron: 'For the generations to come none of your descendants who has a defect may come near to offer the food of his God. No man who has any defect may come near: no man who is blind or lame, disfigured or deformed. (Leviticus 21:17-18)*

Now, I know that you and your Super-Christians (*praise be to Super-Jesus*), who speak in tongues (like I used to do in drama class in early high school...just saying...), who denounce abortion, homosexuality and who fear Super-Satan who lurks around every corner, have all but abolished the Old Testament. You protest that your old mate Jesus-the-Jew had absolved you of the 'old laws'. So why then, are you and your fruit-cake friends, who no longer believe that the Old Testament laws are binding, taking so damn much offence to other people not observing Old Testament laws? Well, this answer is pretty easy; you're complete, total and utter freaking hypocrites! You pick and choose the bits and pieces of the Bible that YOU BELIVE BEST SUIT YOUR OWN CAUSE, ignore the rest, and then use your focused material to justify perpetrating hate crimes against the gays!

I suppose the real question is, should I be surprised? Seriously, in America, we've seen Christianity spawn some seriously dangerous, violent and bigoted cults, the KKK, Doomsday/Apocalypse Religious Cults, the American Nazis, Aryan Nation, and many, many more. All of these cults use the Bible to justify their attacks on Jews, on Blacks, on Mexicans and people of other backgrounds. They take the words from the Bible, twist them to meet their own needs/ends to go out and paint the town red... with other people's blood.

I've always said there is no such thing as a Progressive or Liberal Christian, just progressive or liberal cherry pickers who have lost touch with Christianity!

Abort! Abort!

Moving along to your next assertion, that "God will not bless a nation where abortion is commonplace", when was it exactly that abortion became *'commonplace'*? Last time I checked the Jaketionary, 'commonplace' referred to things such as riding a bike on a sunny day, playing with your kids in the park and walking your dog. When exactly did 'terminating a mass of multiplying cells' become 'commonplace'?

What an unbelievably arbitrary statement for you to have made!

People, for whatever reason, listen to you Pat; they listen to what you and the other bigoted, intolerant figureheads of Christianity have to say, and react in the exact same way that Muslims listen to their bigoted, intolerant figureheads. So many religious sheep!

What disgusts me is that you have this great big view of abortion being such a horrible and murderous act, but could not care less about the actual life that the child will have, once it is born. Growing up as a mistake that your mother made when she was 16 would be a really, really tough act. But you couldn't care less about how well or [more likely] how poorly this new child will be cared and provided for, and as studies have shown many times over, the same situation that the child is born into is most likely to be repeated.

While the Christian moral-legion is picketing abortion clinics on your orders, Pat, children are being neglected; they're sitting in orphanages; they're being abused and neglected by Moms and Dads; foster families; church officials; priests and pastors. They're living in dangerous family dynamics and in poverty with little or no hope of finding their way out, ever.

I'm not saying that these children would be better off not existing, but you need to acknowledge, Pat, that the decision to go through with a pregnancy is just as difficult as the decision to terminate one. I am certainly not saying that the women who terminate today won't be great mothers in the future either, but you can not expect a teenager to give up their *entire* lifestyle, forego *all* opportunities for a stable and productive life for their future, and live with the *millions* of other teenage mothers on the verge of poverty, for one stupid mistake (which is unlikely to be taken lightly after the abortion).

My point is this, your Christian minions spend so much time and energy denouncing abortion because of your preconceived notion that 'life starts at conception', but simply do not care about what happens when the child is born.

The decision to terminate forces the girl to contemplate her decisions and weigh them against her future and it leaves an emotional 'scar' that will stay with her for the rest of her life. For abortion to be referred to as "common place" is to say that it is a decision that is easy to come by, this is ultimately an ignorant and deeply hurtful statement.

Women who terminate pregnancies do not do so in the name of conquest of land, they do so to ensure that a stupid decision doesn't ruin the rest of their lives and that of their progeny, if they were to have been born.

So Gay

You next infer that 'homosexuality is institutionalized'. This is another completely arbitrary statement and clearly illustrates how deeply your bigotry runs. Homosexuality is not a 'condition' or a 'disease' that one can catch. The very fact that homosexuality has been observed in a multitude of animal species alive today - including that of the primates with which we are closely genetically linked - should tell you that the human animal is no different.

But how do you even begin to extrapolate 'institutionalized homosexuality'? I assume that you are referring to how children are now no longer taught to be actively bigoted towards homosexuals in their community, am I right? Well, were you giving a similar speech when, in a similar way 'Blacks were institutionalized'?

While I don't particularly want to relate the plight of the African-Americans post slavery with Homosexuality, I do want to make the following point; African-Americans are people and deserve every right that white people deserve. Homosexuals, Lesbians, Transgender and Intersex people, are people also and deserve every right that strait people deserve. It is not homosexuality that is being institutionalized; it is bigotry, as much as it was racism in the past that is being de-institutionalized.

All you do is demonstrate just how much your religion serves to segregate. "Peace and Love", my ass! You don't want peace, you want subservience; you don't want love, and you want slavery.

Pray For Me

For the longest time, Pat, those who were not of your particular sect of Christianity have had to send their children to schools where lies were taught as fact by teachers that were trusted by children. So when you and your fellow bible-bashers cry foul that prayer and Bible reading are being taken out of public schools, I shed a faux tear as the world's smallest violin plays the 'Walking Away' theme from the Hulk.

Seriously Pat, I'm so sorry that the only place that you Christians have to pray now is your home, your church, your cars, your buses and everywhere else that is conceivable. Do you seriously think that you're going to get a good result out of forcing children to pray to a God that they didn't choose, for a religion that their parents indoctrinated them into? When you force a child to pray, you are not forcing them to be good; you're forcing them to conform to your narrow view of the world.

Worse still, when good parents ask for their child to be excused from such pointless filth as mandatory prayer and Bible reading, all that happens is that the child is ostracized for no other reason than wanting a bloody choice. In another letter, I've examined the futility of prayer, and unless you're hoping to teach the children about the horrors of the God of the Old Testament, who openly murdered everything from children to animals in the name of conquest for his Hebrew people, then reading the Bible will teach them nothing either. Especially the subjective teaching that you are so darn good at!

In the Old Testament, God killed around 30 million men, women - some of whom would have inevitably been pregnant - and children, all in the name of placing his people, the Hebrews/Jews/12 Tribes at the top of the heap, yet you worship Him. How could you denounce women for terminating a pregnancy when your own God - whose convoluted and twisted words you use to denounce said abortion - committed bloody murder in the name of conquest.

The Courts Are Against God

You say, "How can we pray for his blessing when we have that going on and when we have courts that have ruled repeatedly against him?" Just in case you're unaware of how courts work, I'll give you a really quick little run-down. Courts rule based on BEST EVIDENCE. Simple enough?

Well, with this in mind, and considering that there is literally NO EVIDENCE OF ANY GOD FROM ANY CIVILISATION THROUGHOUT HISTORY, it is completely impossible for a 'court to rule against God' as there is no evidence to support it's existence.

Consider that you, as you claim, make decisions and carry out actions based on your assertion that your god, the God of the Jews, exists. I mean, you obviously don't make any decisions based on signs from the Greek God Zeus, or the Roman God Jupiter, or the Egyptian God Ra, do you? You don't have any reason or evidence to support the existence of those Gods, despite the ancient Greeks, Romans and Egyptians historical beliefs and based on that distinct lack of evidence, you don't believe in them, right Pat?

Well, given the distinct lack of evidence for your god, it would be pretty stupid, let alone negligent, for the courts to rule based on your assertion that such a thing exists, regardless of whether you, or anyone else claims to be an 'authority' on the subject.

When a child makes an imaginary friend, they talk to it, play with it and for the most part, you let them have fun, chuckle about having a creative child and trust that they'll grow out of it, right? So, Pat, why shouldn't you be put in a mental institution for claiming that your imaginary friend is talking to you? You don't have any evidence to support its existence, and sure, I don't have any existence to prove that it doesn't exist, but that most certainly doesn't support your claim that such things exist.

No amount of people believing in something that does not exist will make that 'thing' exist. The same applies to your god.

Moreover, one should not invest in a belief system based on the assertion that if they don't, they endure torture in Hell. We went to Iraq to liberate the Iraqis from just that, so you cannot justify it in the case of religious belief.

What would life have been like if you'd won the presidency in 1988?

An Abomination

You say, "Now we have perversion which God calls abomination". One minute it's what "you" call and abomination, and the next minute it is what "God" calls an abomination, which is the real authority, Pat? And what do you mean by "now"? If you've read your Bible, you ass-hat, there were two cities renowned for their bum-fun way back in the very beginning of the Old Testament, Sodom and Gomorrah! Ring any bells, mate?

If you've got a handle on that now, you might as well admit that, by your standards – i.e. the universe is only 5-10,000 years old – abomination is as old as the universe. As I said above, homosexuality has been observed in almost every animal species alive today, certainly in mammals though. Furthermore, there is every reason to suspect that homosexuality in nature has occurred since sexual reproduction began, as it is our hormones that drive us to sex. Even in the animal world, mammals have sex just for the sake of having sex... wouldn't you?

Bankruptcy
Your statement about the country ultimately going bankrupt is probably true, but it is not a case of divine retribution that is driving it. No, rather it is a president who exhausted the Federal Reserve with his own personal Holy Crusade, then backed it up by deregulating the finance and banking sectors. Make no mistake Pat, the president who you endorsed twice, was personally responsible for driving the world economy to its knees. To top that, his little crusade in the Holy Land continues indefinitely at huge detriment to the USA, both in terms of finance (several trillion dollars) and in loss of American lives.

Now you finally have a president who wants to do something meaningful for the American people and provide healthcare to all and he's got no money and no support to do it with.

As for moral bankruptcy, well, parts of America have been cesspools of violence and objective evil for decades; the country its self was forged through a hard fought, bloody civil war. If you want to fix this problem, you only need look towards the plethora of studies into overwhelming influence that education plays. To be clear, when I refer to education, I am talking about engaging education, not just facts and textbooks. If the education doesn't engage the kid, they won't want to attend. Those same studies that promote social change through education also infer that the type of education one receives plays a part in how receptive they are to it.

Unfortunately, kids are faced with schools where teachers are not completely educated on the subjects they teach. The direct consequence of this is that the children cannot ask a question of their teacher and expect that it will be answered, so they stop asking (if they're not directly told to shut-up first).

Of course, Bush's "No Child Gets Left Behind" legislation certainly helped to ensure that the schools that really needed to be able to afford good quality educators, experienced and academically enthused teachers, couldn't. Hey, didn't you personally endorse Bush twice, Pat? Ah, sorry I already said that...

Your closing words are filled with joy and affluence for the future; "I would love to say the Lord told me it's going to be peace and prosperity and it's wonderful and that God's going to bless America, he's going to bless you, he's going to bless your business, you're going to make a lot of money in the stock market and everybody's going to be happy. I can't say that."

What a consummate optimist you are, Pat! Why is it that you evangelicals get so down on life when you believe quite loudly that life is in fact only temporary? What's with that anyway? If you truly believe that Heaven will contain far more splendor than your time on Earth, why the hell don't you just get it over with and take the shotgun express outta here?

I have to be honest, Pat, I think we'd be far better off without you.

Yours in infamy,

Jake Farr-Wharton

TO KEN HAM

Made in China
– Creationism

Dear Reader, the following is an article by Ken Ham, the president and founder of Answers in Genesis-U.S. and the Creation Museum (with over 719,000 visitors in its first two years). He has become one of the most in-demand Christian conference speakers and talk show guests. Ken is the author of many books on Genesis, including *Already Gone*, co-authored by renowned researcher Britt Beemer on why so many young people have left the church, the best-selling *The Lie: Evolution*, and a number of children's books (*Dinosaurs of Eden, D is for Dinosaur, A is for Adam*, etc.) The full address can be found here:

www.answersingenesis.org/articles/am/v2/n3/science-or-the-bible

In this ongoing war between creation and evolution, Christians are always looking for the strongest evidence for creation. They are looking for the "magic bullet" that will prove to their evolutionist friends that creation is true and evolution is false.

The Bible's account of beginnings cannot be tested in a laboratory, so secular scientists—and even some Christians—believe it is not science and must be classified as religion.

Creationists and evolutionists, Christians and non-Christians, all have the same evidence—the same facts. Think about it: we all have the same earth, the same fossil layers, the same animals and plants, the same stars—the facts are all the same.

Secular scientists claim that their view of beginnings (evolution) can be tested in a laboratory, so their view is scientific. For instance, they point to mutated fruit flies or speciation observed in the field (such as new species of mosquitoes or fish).

But this is where many people are confused—what is meant by "science" or "scientific."

Although there are other uses of the word, the root meaning of science is basically "knowledge." In fact, in the past, philosophy and theology were considered sciences, and theology was even called the "queen of the sciences."

But over the past 200 years, during the so-called Scientific Revolution, the word science has come to mean a method of knowing, a way of discovering truth. Moreover, many people assume that modern science is the only way to discover truth.

Both creationist scientists and evolutionist scientists have religious (or faith) components to their scientific models about origins. Yet both types of scientists are equally capable of doing both operation science and origin science.

So, how was the Grand Canyon formed? Was it formed gradually over long periods of time by a little bit of water, or was it formed rapidly by a lot of water? The first interpretation is based on secular assumptions of slow change over millions of years, while the second interpretation is based on biblical assumptions about rapid change during Noah's Flood.

Of course, evolutionary scientists can test their interpretations using operation science. For instance, evolutionists point to natural selection and speciation—which are observable today. Creation scientists make these same observations, but they recognize that the change has limits and has never been observed to change one kind into another.

The Bible, in contrast, is the eyewitness testimony of the Creator, who tells us what happened to produce the earth, the different kinds of life, the fossils, the rock layers, and indeed the whole universe. The Bible gives us the true, "big picture" starting assumptions for origin science.

Creationists and evolutionists develop totally different reconstructions of history. But they accept and use the same methods of research in both origin and operation science. The different conclusions about origins arise from different starting assumptions, not the research methods themselves.

Many people believe fossils and/or fossil-bearing layers were formed over millions of years ... but is this true? Or are many of the 'billions of dead things buried in rock layers laid down by water all over the Earth' the result of the Flood of Noah's day, which occurred just a few thousand years ago? Dead animals left alone will rot or be consumed by scavengers. Fossilization requires rapid, catastrophic events.

So, the battle between the Bible and molecules-to-man evolution is not one of religion versus science. Rather, it is a conflict between worldviews—a creationist's starting assumptions (a biblical worldview) and an evolutionist's starting assumptions (an antibiblical worldview).

Dear Ken,

Firstly, I just wanted to comment on how much I like your website. I really love the 'intelligence rating' system that you've used to categorize each of the articles. They range from "Layman" in an appealing green color to "Technical" in a scary red color. For proponents of the creation science and intelligent design movement, I imagine this rating system comes in very handy because when you're dealing with evolution, the last thing you want is to be bogged down by nasty 'technical' words and hard to grasp 'facts'.

I really enjoy reading your overt criticisms of atheism, evolution and all religions other than fundamentalist Christianity. To me it shows that the messages of intolerance and supremacy and segregation based on religious (specific deity) belief that were fostered by the original architects of the Bible are alive and well today. What does disgust me, however, is that your teachings against biological evolution by way of natural selection are delivered to around one million people each year (and growing).

What really worries me though, Ken, is just how many children you are preaching creationism to. I'm not a warm and fuzzy atheist like so many others today, I am not willing to sit down and shut up while you literally brainwash children into believing what you claim to be the 'truth' of universal origin. I've watched your documentaries and listened to your podcast and as such, I've seen and heard children in your audience agreeing with you as your weave a crafty string of faith based reasoning into inferred truth of biblical genesis. For your Layman friends, put simply, you make it sound like you would have to be stupid to believe in science and evolution, or for the Creationists in the audience, you make the smart people look dumb and the dumb people look smart. This is brainwashing, plain and simple.

When you teach a child that science is wrong for not teaching from the Bible, you are teaching them to live with Bronze Age intelligence 4000 years after the Bronze Age ended. Biblical genesis has been completely refuted, so why teach it as fact? Why teach a child that the misguided philosophical ramblings of the nomadic desert tribes from 4-5000 years ago are anything more than historical philosophy?

Instead of attempting to understand evolution, you ridicule it and in doing so, you pollute the minds of millions of adults and their children. Genesis is factually wrong; get over it before you do some real damage.

We're at War

War is often a beautifully evocative word, which I think is ultimately overstated in this context of evolution versus creationism. It's fine that you've chosen to use it, though it doesn't make me think you're any less of an ass-hat. If you wish to think of it as a war, evolution should be thought of as an army of ever growing, intelligent and diligent soldiers armed with ever developing super technology, versus a large group of rednecks using paperclips shaped to look like machine guns and a belief that they have telekinetic powers. Analogically, it is wolves (evolution) versus grumpy Cockroaches (creation).

On a side note, did you know that cockroaches are able to live for up to a week after being decapitated? I say this not as any sort of veiled threat, but as an illustration of the wonder of evolution. A trait such as being able to survive decapitation in order to complete a reproductive cycle is one of those obvious things that would be favored by natural selection. If you can survive to pass on your DNA, then such a trait can, and obviously did, prevail. I digress.

It is true, as you say, that Creationist Christians are always looking for their 'magic bullet' that you can use to debunk evolution, but again, you're using Bronze Age philosophy to debunk proven scientific theory. If you really want to do something special, why don't you get together and go to Holy Land and search for the Holy Grail or the Arc of the Covenant killing everything that gets in your way during your pursuit. Call it something like a 'Holy Crusade'!

The fact of the matter is that there literally is no 'magic bullet'; evolution explains our origins, and biblical genesis makes a fairytale out of it. Biblical genesis isn't even a fairytale, because the moral of the several stories are simplified as do or say anything against this supposed ethereal overlord, God, and he'll mess you up. Then if you add a bit of New Testament philosophy into the story it becomes do or say anything against God and he'll commit you to torture for all eternity. Nothing says unconditional love like infinite punishments for finite crimes.

Sciency Stuff

You tell your first lie in paragraph two though Ken, when you say that the Bible's account of 'beginnings cannot be tested in a laboratory'. Laboratories, along with the observations he made on his well-documented expeditions, were, in fact, integral to expanding on Darwin's theory of Natural Selection, which lays a strong foundation for biological evolution. As such, it is quite easy to test the Bible's account of beginnings in the laboratory.

3.7 billion years ago, in what scientists' term 'primordial earth', the conditions were turbulent. Mostly wet, very warm and with an atmosphere filled with all sorts of gases, the most abundant of which were hydrogen, hydrogen-cyanide, ammonium and methane. In 1961, Hydrogen, Cyanide and Ammonium were left to stew in a high-pressure environment with 'tidal pools', similar to the primordial earth. After some time and left untouched, the three gases produced amino acids, the oh-so-important nucleotides that make up a DNA sequence.

In the 1980's, scientists found a particular type of clay, Montmorillonite, which was abundant in the sea floor and in hot pools of water on land during the primordial earth. This actually formed the perfect catalyst for forming polynucleotide, or long chains that would eventually form RNA. These polynucleotide chains would acquire specific traits over time to better suit their environment.

Over hundreds of millions of years, RNA grew more and more complex, a single strand formed a second strand and DNA was born. Now, the major difference between RNA and DNA is that DNA requires proteins or amino acids to replicate. Luckily, the same Montmorillonite stew that formed the nucleotides was abundant all sorts of complex chemicals such as amino acids and one of those chemicals, lipids, has a natural tendency to form into spherical structures called micelles.

RNA or DNA that attracted these lipid molecules would have been better protected inside the micelle structure and as such, had a better ability to survive and replicate more successfully. Here we have a primitive single cell organism doing nothing more than surviving. The rest (i.e. the next 3.7 billion years) is history.

While neither of the 1961 or 1980 cases empirically proves that what happened in their controlled experiments was what occurred here on our Earth, it does show that there is a viable model for explaining our origin from nothing, to something.

When you couple this explanation of with a fossil record showing a fabulous progression of many different species to present day humanity and the study of genomics, which illustrates that journey, it is pretty clear that you can call Biblical Genesis, refuted. Which means that there was no Adam and Eve, no eating of the Tree of Knowledge and no original sin.

Saint Paul's assertion therefore, that Jesus' selfless act of sacrifice to cleanse the world original and future sin is beautiful bullshit. What this means is that the Jesus character in the Bible is irrelevant, or at least irrelevant to all future generations. He might have annoyed the ruling Hebrews/Jews during his time, and he might have pissed off the Romans, but to you and me, he's just a hyped up myth.

Fact or Crap

It is true, as you say, that "Creationists and evolutionists, Christians and non-Christians, all have the *same* evidence — the same facts", the difference lies in where we take these facts. A paleontologist, might take these fossils or layers of sediment etc. and have them dated, and try to link them to the already established fossil record. Creationists, on the other hand, you take a fossil of a dinosaur for example, you stick them in your creation museums and you try to make it seem as though they fit within your notion of a 5-7000 year old planet and universe.

Personally, I love the (primarily creationist) assertion that dinosaur fossils were strategically placed as a test to ensure that only the true Christian's made it into Heaven. I hope they realize then that Heaven is going to be filled with rednecks, idiots and cretins! On the bright side though, all of history's greatest minds will be in Hell, engineering a method to get into Heaven and wreck up the place!

When the answer of how old the dinosaur fossils actually are is released to the public, the paleontologist rejoices at having found another link between one species and the next whilst the creationist publicly denounces the scientist for 'speaking out against God.' Truth be told, it is utterly irrelevant whether the creationist believes in the findings or not, they just miss out on being a part of the long and exciting journey of scientific discovery!

It seems implausible to me that God would create an infinite number of species of dinosaurs, just to kill them, burry them in hundreds of millions of years worth of rock and earth, just to confuse proponents of a particular field of science in 2000 A.D.! It is far more likely that Genesis, as much as the notion of gods is the product of early humanity's very best attempt to explain their origins using their newly acquired cognitive powers of logic and reason. They made an incredible effort considering the tools at their disposal... but why are we still following their musing?

You then say that 'secular scientists claim that their view of beginnings can be tested in a laboratory, so their view is scientific', and indeed, you are correct. Also, it is not just species such as the fruit fly where evolution can be observed.

Twenty years ago, evolutionary biologist Richard Lenski of Michigan State University in East Lansing, US, took a single strain Escherichia coli (E.Coli – i.e. the 'special ingredient' in the late night kebab you ate after clubbing all night that gave you a terrible case of the squirts) bacterium and used its descendants to found 12 laboratory populations. The 12 have been growing ever since, gradually accumulating mutations and evolving for more than 44,000 generations, while Lenski watches what happens. All colonies were exposed to different conditions, heat, cold, humidity etc. and unsurprisingly, they adapted.

Mostly, the patterns Lenski saw were similar in each separate population. All 12 evolved larger cells, for example, as well as faster growth rates on the glucose they were fed, and lower peak population densities. But sometime around the 31,500th generation, something dramatic happened in just one of the populations – the bacteria suddenly acquired the ability to metabolize citrates, a second nutrient in their culture medium that E. coli normally cannot metabolize - in fact, that characteristic is usually used to distinguish that particular strain of E. coli from others. They evolved.

Kapow!

Christian Crapology

I assume you're referring specifically to creationist Christians when you refer to 'many people' being confused by science and scientific. Even the Christians I know can tell the difference between nouns (Science) and adjectives (Scientific).

Now, Ken, there is a reason why philosophy and theology were described as "the queen of the sciences", this is because in ancient times, theology and philosophy were the only tools available to humanity to explain our origins. When this was done, philosophy and theology set about divining and attributing some inherent purpose to humanity.

Philosophy and theology have their place in our history. They once held great importance in the exchange of moral obligations, tradition and conduct from one generation to the next. Parables and stories of great battles were, for the longest time, the best way of teaching successive generations lessons learned by the preceding ones. Philosophy still plays some part in societal ethics. Theology, on the other hand, is obsolete. Theology no longer has anything of importance or relevance to teach us that we can't learn from any Dr Seuss book. Have you ever read, "The Bug That Went 'Kachoo'"? It is a great way for children to learn 'Cause and Effect'.

It's History

You refer to the scientific revolution as being 200 years old, but if you want to talk about science refuting biblical inaccuracy, you can go back even further. Nicolaus Copernicus, born 1473, was the first astronomer to formulate a comprehensive heliocentric cosmology (i.e. the discovery that the Earth and all planets in the solar system, rotated around a larger body, the sun) that refuted the Bible's and the ruling Christian bodies at the time's claims that the Earth was the centre of the universe. Galileo Galilei, born 1564, has been called the "father of modern observational astronomy," the "father of modern physics," the "father of science," and "the Father of Modern Science." Stephen Hawking says, "Galileo, perhaps more than any other single person, was responsible for the birth of modern science."

Both of these great men were held back by the Christians of their day. Unfortunately, while you new evangelical Christians claim to be completely removed from Catholic dogma, your methods and madness are exactly the same. When a new, revolutionary way of thought comes to light, when the doors of reason are opened, you grab your pitch fork and torches, forcefully nail those doors shut and then urinate all over them so as to leave your mark... which is very naughty, dogs (Canis lupus familiaris) and Homo sapiens diverged from our common ancestors 98.2 million years ago (*www.timetree.org*)!

Science has historically been persecuted by Christianity. By persecuted, I mean *actually* persecuted, not 'Christian persecuted'. The Christians that cry persecution every time someone questions their silly dogma are a fickle bunch. They're the soccer players of the religious world, appealing for a penalty with a broken ankle every time someone near them sneezes.

It's Pronounced 'Creation Mythscience'

You next say that, "both creationist scientists and evolutionist scientists have religious (or faith) components to their scientific models about origins", but this is just a logical fallacy that you've used to support your convoluted viewpoint. The theorem comprising evolution does not require religious faith, let alone any other types of faith, at all, because it is testable, observable and it is reproducible which means that at no point to you have to take a leap of faith in order to quantify it. On the other hand, in order to believe in biblical genesis, not only do you have cover your eyes and your ears and shout "LALALALALA-I'm Not Listening" really loudly, but you also have to take a massive leap to believe in a celestial sky-pixie.

If you were a Hebrew and lived in Old Testament times, you wouldn't have needed to make the 'leap of faith' in order to believe in biblical genesis. After all, there were plenty of people who met with God in the OT and God directly acted on behalf of his chosen people to destroy their enemies and opposition. Problem is, we have the direct descendants of that civilization, the present day Jews, who were utterly decimated in both the crusades of the Middle Ages and more recently, in the Holocaust. All throughout their suffering, God was apparently totally unwilling to directly intervene and alter the plight of his *chosen people*. Hitler didn't even get as much as a bad case of hemorrhoids.

Rocks and Stuff

How was the Grand Canyon formed, Ken? You say that you think that it was the result of Noah's biblical flood, but did you know that the Great Pyramid of Cheops was built about 2589-2566 BC, about 230 years before the flood was reputed to have happened, yet it has no water marks on it. The Djoser Step Pyramid at Saqqara, Egypt, built about 2630 BC doesn't show any signs of having been under water. Likewise for many other ancient structures.

The Egyptians also have continuous historical records for hundreds of years before and after the 'time of the flood that' and have absolutely no records of a flood of epic proportion *ever* occurring. The significance of this is, of course, that the Egyptians were on the continent at and around the same elevation as the ancient Hebrews and were not only *not aware* of a global flood, but also not affected by one; this completely refutes the Biblical Flood.

Outside of the Bible, there is no evidence that would place a continental flood, let alone a worldwide one, during the time period specified by the Bible. As such, it would be absolutely stupid to assert that such a thing occurred in any form beyond myth.

As you say though, evolutionary scientists and ~~complete morons~~ creation scientists have access to the same observations and will make their own conclusions based on what they have learned, *or* in the case of creation scientists, were indoctrinated to believe.

In my mind though, this cannot be true. After all, biological evolution by way of natural selection, as discussed above, has been demonstrated empirically. The only thing that has inhibited our observation of it in a laboratory is that it literally takes tens or sometimes hundreds of thousands of generations in order to exhibit a noticeable difference. Obviously, in normal situations, this would be impossible to have observed any changes in our species. This is why the E. Coli bacteria evolution was such a massive discovery.

Ken, your creation science friends 'recognize that observed evolution has limits' are indoctrinated to believe just that. The Bible is not, and never has been an 'eyewitness testimony of the Creator', it is the misguided ramblings of Bronze Age desert nomads, nothing more. By misguided, I mean that they had no foundation in which to properly uncover their origins. This ability would not come for another several thousand years (i.e. the age of enlightenment).

The Bible, especially the Old Testament tells some seriously far-fetched tales of super human feats. In the story Noah's Ark, you have a senior citizen who builds a seaworthy boat, big enough to hold two of every land dwelling species on Earth *and* with enough leftover space for food for forty days adrift. This same senior citizen would also have needed to traverse the entire globe to collect the land dwellers (Koala, what the hell is a Koala?). The Bible also says that Noah lived for 900 years and he and his family would have had to repopulate the entire Earth.

The alleged repopulation of the Earth is completely refuted by reproductive science. When you consider the severity of the inbreeding required for Noah and his family to repopulate the earth, the chance of such a claim being even slightly possible is blown out the window.

Unfortunately, what the authors of the Bible did not know is that inbreeding causes *severely* reduced fertility in each successive generation. Ken, while you and your creationist friends may claim that this wouldn't have mattered because Noah had several sons who had already taken wives, the problem of inbred offspring infertility is shared throughout the animal kingdom... i.e. every one of those animal's offspring's offspring would have had sincere difficulty reproducing.

What I find hard to comprehend, Ken, is that refuting the claim of an actual biblical flood only took a few hours of research in science journals (who had done the exhaustive research for me). So why the hell would you spend your entire life preaching that Noah and his flood, and all of the ludicrous stories from the Bible are true when the evidence to the contrary is insurmountable?

Furthermore, the Old Testament stories aren't even good parables. The moral of every single parable in the Old Testament is, "piss of God and you're screwed!" At least the 'Boy Who Cried Wolf' and 'The Tortoise and the Hare' provide you with messages that make you think. Anything from Dr Seuss also teaches a lighthearted lesson on morality.

No such luck for the Hebrews though, all they had was 'God doesn't like bum sex, so do it and he'll blow up your city' (Sodom & Gomorrah), 'God doesn't like people having fun, so enjoy life and he'll drown the Earth' (Noah's flood), and 'sending your virgin daughters to be raped by a crowd is preferable to allowing said crowd to rape two strangers you just met' (Lot). Seriously Ken, you teach kids to believe that Noah's flood is real, but a) there is NO EVIDENCE TO SUPPORT IT, b) there is INSURMOUNTABLE CONTRARY EVIDENCE, c) there is NO PROLIFIC MORAL TO THE STORY and d) SUCH ASSERTIONS ARE MORONIC!

History

You say, "Creationists and evolutionists develop totally different reconstructions of history" and again this is true. The proponent of evolution recognizes that history is an open book, just waiting to be written as we traverse the universe uncovering our origins and indeed our potential future. In contrast, the proponent of creation recognizes that history is a book written by our ancestors in a time where the wheel was an emerging technology.

For evolution, there are plenty of gaps to be filled and so many exciting mind expanding adventures lay ahead for us to fill those gaps. For creation, everything that is worth knowing about our origins was written 4,000 years before DNA was discovered.

Simple science, chemistry, physics and astronomy tell us that the bits of matter that comprise every living thing on this planet are traceable to stars in far off galaxies. As Carl Sagan said, "we are star dust, contemplating the stars". Life in this universe is not the result of some celestial overlord exerting its will; it is the product of billions of years of cause and effect, of trial and error and of natural selection.

Every century, our eyes are opened anew to and endless superfluity of possibilities. Religion, especially that of creationism, seeks only to revert our understanding of our universe to that of the Bronze Age. Every century, scientific pursuit has been met with malicious opposition from fools like yourself, Ken, who believe that they have the answer to every question worth asking, ever.

Billions of Dead Things

You next claim that the "billions of dead things buried in rock layers laid down by water all over the Earth" are the result of the Flood of Noah's day, which occurred just a few thousand years ago. You say, "dead animals left alone will rot or be consumed by scavengers, but fossilization requires rapid, catastrophic events." While it is mostly true that fossilization requires rapid and catastrophic events (in some cases), it is utterly naïve to refer to this as being the result of a flood from only a few thousand years ago.

In fact, the easiest way to refute this is to look at DNA. A fossil of up to around 100,000 years can still contain proteins, making it possible for DNA extraction to take place. Even so, at this 100,000-year cut off period, the proteins are incomplete as they break down slowly over time. Fossils that originate from anywhere between a few thousand years upwards have plenty of material available for DNA extraction (when properly preserved). As such, Ken, if dinosaurs were fossilized as the result of a global flood only a few thousand years ago instead of a meteorite 65 million years ago, we should be able to extract DNA from their specimens.

The inability to extract DNA from dinosaur fossils recovered from any of the thousands of sites across the globe certainly corroborates the evidence suggesting that the earth is in fact 4.45 billion years old. This differs widely from the creationist assertion that the earth is only a few thousand years old. Actually, I'm pretty sure that this justifies my ridicule of you and your silly little friends throughout this letter. Did I say silly? Is that even strong enough? Is it comprehensive enough?

As such Ken, I believe we have proven once again that to believe and teach children the idea that the fossilized remains of dinosaurs are the result a global flood is literally despotic because a) there is NO EVIDENCE TO SUPPORT IT, b) there is INSURMOUNTABLE CONTRARY EVIDENCE, c) there is NO PROLIFIC MORAL TO THE STORY and d) SUCH ASSERTIONS ARE MORONIC!

Back to The War

Unfortunately for you, Ken, the war or battle between the biblical genesis and 'molecules-to-man evolution' as you put it, is not a conflict between worldviews based on assumptions. The battle is between quantified and verified scientific theorem and a guess from a book for delusional stupid people. Between FACT AND FICTION!

I'm not being asinine to belittle you either, Ken, that is just a secondary benefit, no, I'm being vindictive to simply illustrate that biblical genesis has been refuted. SO STOP TEACHING IT TO CHILDREN, YOU ARE RETARDING THEIR INTELLECTUAL DEVELOPMENT!

If you want to teach children fairy tales like Noah's Ark, the Jewish Exodus from Egypt, or Jesus' resurrection into Heaven, then teach it as the fairy tale that it is. Maybe add in a unicorn, a dragon and a princess... whoops, they're already in there!

My dear Ken, before I say farewell, I would like to make an appeal to your better judgment. Anyone familiar with evolution, and any field of science for that matter, understands that it is not infallible, and that in a manner of speaking, is evolving its self. Obviously, the theory isn't growing a hard shell to protect from the talons of creationists, but it is continually gathering new evidence to expand on the theory. More transitional fossils, more missing links, more hominids, more beautiful, interesting and utterly exhilarating discoveries; this is what science has delivered to us and what it is likely to continue to do for millennia to come (IF we can move past these pointless religious divisions).

Biblical genesis will forever be the same feeble attempt at understanding our origins that it always has been.

One day we may well have a theory for 'everything', one that we can use to understand and validate literally everything. Even now, with only five hundred odd years of scientific enlightenment on our side, we are learning at unprecedented and enthralling rates. Our accumulated knowledge is quickly becoming a solid foundation for wisdom for generations to come. Don't build your metaphorical house on the sand of stupidity, Ken... alas, I dare say you already have – the color coding system on your articles from ignoramus to creation scientist level (is there a distinction in that?) speaks volumes!

Creation Science and Intelligent Design does nothing but hold humanity back. You wrongly assume that the Bible holds the answers to the universe when it clearly does not. By teaching children that biblical genesis or creation is a real and valid theory and that science and evolution is wrong, all you are doing is passing your torch of ignorance to yet another generation.

In a perfect Darwinian world, these intellectually stunted individuals would not be able to pass the stupid-gullible gene onto the next generation. The evolution-deniers would be ostracized and ridiculed, thought of as nothing more than the crazy troglodyte conspiracy theorists that they literally are. Alas that is not the case, they are valued within their evolution-denying communities, they travel, they have babies and they 'teach the controversy' to the next generation.

Your only requirement for proof of God's existence, and thus proof of your creation, is the existence of the Bible. You claim the Bible to have been written by people who purportedly conversed with God, thus God created the Bible and the Bible is a testament to God's existence. Circular reasoning. The logic behind the Creationist argument is thus: Hypothesis - Darwin is wrong; Experiment - Read the Holy Bible; Results - God said it, I believe it.

What I find most arrogant is that you claim that the holes in big-bang theory and evolution theory are the flaws that prove the Bible true, for it has answers where science does not. We're a young species, Ken, we've already found our biological origin, and give it some more time and maybe we'll visit the crucible of the universe.

Isn't it time that you grew up? Isn't it time that you stop blaming evolution for being so damn hard to understand?

Ultimately, Intelligent Design, Fundamentalism, Creation Science and every religion that believes that such assertions are viable alternatives to evolution, comes down to a simple economic formula: Getting an education is expensive, being an utterly vacant, ignorant, arrogant, bigoted, ass-hat, idiot is free. Not that I'd suggest that you were any of those.

Yours in Science,

Jake Farr-Wharton

Afterword

I want you to consider this afterword as a form of disclaimer (though it most certainly isn't). Do not take anything that I've said in these letters as gospel truth. I've researched every topic exhaustively and have presented for you the best evidence available, but DO NOT take my word for it, do the research yourself and draw your own conclusions.

I was once and for a very long period of time a Christian fundamentalist. I was taught that evolution was a myth; that bad people go to Hell; and not to think for tomorrow for we were in the 'end times'. It took me many years of horrible depression, of toil and deprogramming to let it go. But I did it.

While it is most certainly true that knowledge is power, knowledge is also incredibly sexy. Learning about this new fact or that one. Finding out about planets in far off solar systems and the methods by which they detect these planets is enthralling!

What about the effect of solar neutrinos on radioactive elements such as gallium?

The information, which we, as a species, have accumulated with the help of some magnificent minds, is just incredible.

Don't grow complacent; don't let these moronic religious leaders take over our education systems, or medical research funding, or university and hospital ethics committees, because they will drive us into the ground.

Don't grow apathetic; no matter how many times you hear the same arguments against secularism and science, you must challenge them and you must help them to see the evidence.

These great big brains that we've evolved over billions of years contain an impressive intelligence. This is the tool for our continued survival as a species.

Learn, teach, love it and pass it on… your brain, and your children, will thank you for it!

I want to finish with a quote from a man who has inspired and driven me:

> *"Recognize that the very molecules that make up your body, the atoms that construct the molecules, are traceable to the crucibles that were once the centers of high mass stars that exploded their chemically rich guts into the galaxy, enriching pristine gas clouds with the chemistry of life. So that we are all connected to each other biologically, to the earth chemically and to the rest of the universe atomically. That's kinda cool! That makes me smile and I actually feel quite large at the end of that. It's not that we are better than the universe; we are part of the universe. We are in the universe and the universe is in us." (Neil deGrasse Tyson)*

About Jake Farr-Wharton

Jake Farr-Wharton, among many other things, is the host of the ImaginaryFriendsShow.com Podcast (The One True Podcast) the best source for science, skepticism, religion/atheism news, current affairs and comedy (not always in that order). Many of the atheist-satire songs featured on the ImaginaryFriendsShow.com podcast have made been featured and are available for sale on iTunes and Amazon.com, among them, "Pray the gay away", and "If you're rapture-ready, say Amen!"

Jake likes to describe himself thus; Freethinker, Naturalist, Anti-theist, LGBT Activist, Secularist, Skeptic, Underpants Enthusiast, Student and Enthusiast of Science, Environmentalist, Humanist, Equality Activist, Husband, Chocolate Lover, Writer, and above all, the worlds sexiest Atheist (self-proclaimed).

Jake has been an active blogger for several years, with over 300 articles written for RustyLime.com.

Join Jake Farr-Wharton on his Facebook page "What Would Jake Do", and the podcast's face book page "The Imaginary Friends Show – Podcast" and follow his twitter ramblings @JakeFarrWharton.

Jake lives in Brisbane, Australia with his wife and two daughters (who have already been promised to Saudi Princes, so don't bother asking).

Further Reading

Sexuality Education IN Texas Public Schools, 2009, *www.tfn.org/site/DocServer/ExecSum-SexReport09.pdf?docID=982*

Poolman EM, Galvani AP (February 2007). *"Evaluating candidate agents of selective pressure for cystic fibrosis"*. Journal of the Royal Society, Interface.

Australia Approves Stem Cell Research on Human Embryos, 2003, *www.worldhealth.net/news/australia_approves_stem_cell_research_on*

Elena, S. F., and R. E. Lenski. 2003. *Evolution experiments with microorganisms: the dynamics and genetic bases of adaptation. Nature Reviews Genetics* 4: 457-469. (Visit the website - *http://myxo.css.msu.edu/ecoli* they've just celebrated the 50,000th generation)

Kitzmiller v. Dover Area School District trial of Intelligent Design:
www.pamd.uscourts.gov/kitzmiller/kitzmiller_342.pdf

Cavicchioli, R. & Thomas, T. 2000. *Extremophiles.* In: J. Lederberg. (ed.) *Encyclopedia of Microbiology, Second Edition, Vol. 2*, pp. 317–337. Academic Press, San Diego.

Schulze-Makuch, Haque, Antonio, Ali, Hosein, Song, Yang, Zaikova, Beckles, Guinan, Lehto, Hallam. *Microbial Life in a Liquid Asphalt Desert.*

Wilson, Z. E. and Brimble, M. A. (January 2009). *"Molecules derived from the extremes of life"*. Nat. Prod. Rep. 26 (1): 44–71. doi:10.1039/b800164m. PMID 19374122

Supernormal Stimuli, Deirdre Barrett, W. W. Norton & Company, 2010

Evolution Rx, Dr William Meller M.D., Perigee Trade, 2009

Death By Black Hole, And Other Cosmic Quandaries Neil deGrasse Tyson, W.W. Norton & Company (New York), 2007

Origins: Fourteen Billion Years of Cosmic Evolution Neil deGrasse Tyson & Donald Goldsmith, W.W. Norton & Company (New York)

A Brief History of Time, Stephen Hawking, Bantam, 1998

The Grand Design, Stephen Hawking, Bantam, 2010

Jesus, Interrupted: Revealing the Hidden Contradictions in the Bible (And Why We Don't Know About Them), Bart D. Ehrman, HarperOne, 2010

Misquoting Jesus: The Story Behind Who Changed the Bible and WhyA Brief History of Almost Everything, Bart D. Ehrman, HarperOne, 2007

Nonsense on Stilts: How to Tell Science from Bunk, Massimo Pigliucci, University Of Chicago Press, 2010

Disproving Christianity: Refuting the World's Most Followed Religion, David G. McAfee, CreateSpace, 2010

God?: A Debate between a Christian and an Atheist, William Lane Craig & Walter Sinnott-Armstrong, Oxford University Press, 2004

The Greatest Show on Earth: The Evidence for Evolution, Richard Dawkins, Free Press, 2010

The Selfish Gene: 30th Anniversary Edition, Richard Dawkins, Oxford University Press, 2006

The God Delusion, Richard Dawkins, Mariner Books, 2008

The Blind Watchmaker: Why the Evidence of Evolution Reveals a Universe without Design, Richard Dawkins, W.W. Norton & Company, 1996

Why People Believe Weird Things: Pseudoscience, Superstition, and Other Confusions of Our Time, Michael Shermer, Holt Paperbacks, 2002

The Demon-Haunted World: Science as a Candle in the Dark, Carl Sagan, Ballantine Books, 1997

50 Reasons People Give for Believing in a God, Guy P. Harrison, Prometheus Books, 2008

The End of Faith: Religion, Terror, and the Future of Reason, Sam Harris, W.W. Norton, 2005

Letter to a Christian Nation, Sam Harris, Vintage, 2008.

God Is Not Great: How Religion Poisons Everything, Christopher Hitchens, Twelve, 2009

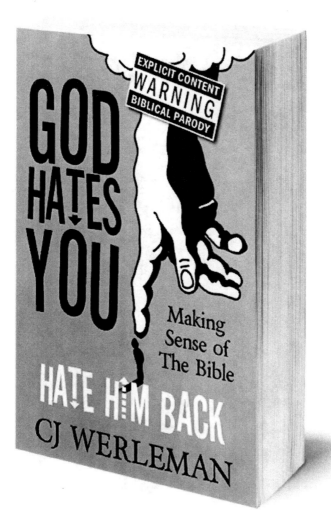

CPSIA information can be obtained at www.ICGtesting.com
230617LV00002B/36/P